D1563376

THE MAGNIFICENT GATEWAY

Sunset view of Shellrock and Wind Mountain intrusions of quartz-diorite (Oregon Dept. of Transp. photo).

SCENIC TRIPS TO THE NORTHWEST'S
GEOLOGIC PAST - NO. 1

THE
MAGNIFICENT
GATEWAY

A Layman's Guide To The

GEOLOGY OF THE
COLUMBIA RIVER GORGE

by

John Eliot Allen

Portland State University

Timber Press, Forest Grove, Oregon

1979

The Magnificent Gateway
John Eliot Allen, Portland State University

©Copyright Timber Press, 1979

ISBN: 0-917304-10-1
Library of Congress catalog card number: 79-2714

Printed in the United States of America

 Timber Press
P.O. Box 92
Forest Grove, Oregon 97116

DEDICATION

This book is dedicated to my wife Margaret, who for forty-five years has unhesitatingly accepted the challenges of over forty uprooting moves dictated by my profession.

The faces of places, and their forms decay;
And that is solid earth, that once was sea;
Seas, in their turn, retreated from the shore,
Make solid land, what ocean was before.

Ovid, *Metamorphoses,* XV (56-117 A.D.)

CONTENTS

Preface ix

Introduction xi

PART I ORIGIN OF THE GORGE 1
CHAPTER 1 HOW GEOLOGY WORKS 1
Geologic words and symbols 3
    Terms used for time............................ 3
    Terms used for rock assemblages 3
    Terms used for rocks 3
    Terms used for structures....................... 8
    Terms used for landforms....................... 10
    Terms used for fossils......................... 10
    Use of geologic symbols 12

Geologic principles and processes 14
    Plate tectonics — the new geology 14
    Internal and external processes.................. 15
    Reconstructing the past........................ 16

Summary of events 17
    Paleocene and Eocene 17
    Oligocene and Miocene......................... 18
    Middle Miocene to Lower Pliocene................ 18
    Middle Pliocene to Present...................... 18

CHAPTER 2 THE NATURAL SETTING 21
The river...................................... 21
The range 23
The Gorge..................................... 24
The weather 27
The trails 29
The vegetation 30

CHAPTER 3 GEOLOGIC HISTORY OF THE GORGE .. 31
The ancient framework 31
The dawn of modern life 33

Continuation of early volcanism 34
The great basalt floods 34
The modern river emerges 39
Fire, ice and flood 44
    Terraces in the Portland area 47
    Faulting and earthquakes in the Gorge area 47
    The catastrophic floods 49
After the ice 52
    Volcanic activity 52
    Landslides 52

CHAPTER 4 MAN IN THE GORGE 59
A capsule history of man in the Gorge 59

PART II HIGHWAY GUIDES 67

CHAPTER 1
HOW TO GET THE MOST OUT OF ROAD LOGS 67
Stratigraphic column 68
Planning the trip 72
Location of Parks 76

CHAPTER 2 GEOLOGIC ROAD LOG: 79
Portland to The Dalles 79

CHAPTER 3 GEOLOGIC ROAD LOG: 111
The Dalles to Vancouver 111

PART III APPENDICES 134

BIBLIOGRAPHY 134

INDEX AND GLOSSARY 139

PREFACE

During the summer of 1931 eleven seniors and graduate students under Dr. E. T. Hodge of the University of Oregon camped in the Columbia River Gorge and around Mount Hood, and for 14 weeks, 7 days a week, mapped the geology of over 2000 square miles north and south of the river between Hood River and Troutdale. I was one of that crew, and spent the ensuing year compiling and plotting the information gained by the party. It is now my pleasure that I can, nearly 50 years later, bring this record up to date. Rocks may not change in one lifetime, but our ideas about them certainly do!

Since that summer the Bonneville and The Dalles dams have submerged the Cascades of the Columbia and the Chutes of The Dalles beneath the waters of their lakes and the I-80 freeway has eliminated the bumper to bumper traffic on the old two-lane "Scenic Highway", but the great black walls of the canyon still rise 3000 feet above the river, and in these walls and tributary canyons are recorded the events which, during the last 40 million years, built and then shaped the mountains, valleys and cliffs, with their pinnacles and waterfalls.

The interpretation of these records in the rock, and the resulting prehistorical account, is the result of contributions made over 60 years by a host of geological workers whose help will be acknowledged along the way.* Especial notice must be made of the pioneer work of Ira A. Williams, who, to celebrate the completion in 1915 of the first paved Columbia River Highway from Portland to Hood River (at the time considered to be one of the great engineering feats of the world), wrote the first extended popular account of the geology of the Gorge.

In preparation for field trips associated with the meeting of the Cordilleran Section of the Geological Society of America in Eugene in March, 1958, I wrote a 23-page "Geologic Field Guide to the Columbia River Gorge" which went through many reprintings as it was used on the annual trip through the Gorge by students from Portland State University. This has been long out of print and out of date, but requests for it still come in. It is hoped that this guidebook may serve as long!

John Eliot Allen, January, 1979

*For a list of supplemental readings, see BIBLIOGRAPHY, on pages 134-8.

INTRODUCTION

"There is something fascinating about science. One gets such wholesale returns of conjecture out of such a trifling investment of fact.

Mark Twain, *Life on the Mississippi"*

Gateway to the Northwest since before the time of Lewis and Clark, the Columbia River Gorge has furnished a pathway for river, railroad, highway and pipeline from the Inland Empire of eastern Oregon and Washington to the West Coast. Sculptured by the mighty Columbia River, second in volume and seventh in length of all rivers in this country, its geologic history may be read not only by the geologist but also by the casual tourist whose visit may originally have been prompted more by the scenic wonders than by the story of the past exhibited in the walls of this great gash through the Cascade Range.

These recorded events began in the late Eocene period of geologic history, some 40 million years ago, and culminated near the end of the Ice Age only a few thousand years ago in catastrophic floods and landslides which were responsible for the present steepness of the canyon walls. Volcanism played a leading role in much of the story, as the river has had to cut its way repeatedly through flows of lava from eastern Oregon; piles of volcanic ash from local volcanoes; and lava dams from volcanoes up tributary valleys. The canyon walls now expose several deep throats of ancient volcanoes. Since the floods, great landslides, some of them still active, have also temporarily dammed the river, doubtless giving rise to the Indian legends of a "Bridge of the Gods."

To the geologist, this "geologic cross-section" through the Cascade Range has been of interest ever since it was studied by Dr. Thomas Condon, pioneer Oregon geologist, who collected fossil leaves from Eagle Creek in 1868. His popular talks throughout the state established a tradition of "letting the public in" on the mysteries and wonders of geology that has carried down to the present among geologists in the Oregon Country, and has resulted in this and many other popular publications on geology (see bibliography).

Chapter 1 of Part I may be skipped over lightly by those who have already been introduced to the science and art of geology. It is an elementary review of those basic principles, processes, ideas and vocabulary which are pertinent to an understanding of the Columbia River Gorge. Chapter 2 is essentially the "geography" of the Columbia River and the Cascade Range which it transects. It also contains "finder" lists, furnishing helpful data on and locations of the waterfalls, pinnacles, and promontories in the Gorge. Chapter 3 attempts to give a fairly detailed frame-by-frame "motion picture" account of the events of the last 40 million years in the northwest, which led to the formation of the present gorge. Part II contains mile-by-mile road logs along the highways on both sides of the river between Portland (and Vancouver) and The Dalles. Hopefully, the appendices, which contain the bibliography of suggested additional readings and the index will also be found of value.

PART I
ORIGIN OF THE GORGE

"The notion of discovering an underlying order in matter is man's basic concept for exploring nature. The architecture of things reveals a structure below the surface, a hidden grain which, when it is laid bare, makes it possible to take natural formations apart ..."

Jacob Bronowski, *The Ascent of Man* (1973)

CHAPTER 1.
HOW GEOLOGY WORKS

Geology is the science of earth. Its chief laboratory is all outdoors. It attempts to answer man's eternal curiosity concerning the Earth he sees around him. The interested amateur can, with only a slight background in the geological sciences, attain a satisfying knowledge of the origin of many of the features he sees. He can learn to recognize the shape of the hills which tells him how they were formed, of valleys and how they were carved. He can recognize the past presence of seas or ice-sheets which once covered parts of the continents.

Deeper appreciation of scenery is only one of the contributions which geology can make to one's enjoyment of life. More important, perhaps, is the realization that the earth today, and all the forms of life which live on its surface and in its seas, are the result of definite although not always well-understood processes, which have been going on for unimaginable eons of time during the development of the earth itself. This unique philosophical contribution of geology can only lead to an appreciation of the time and space that is essential for any comprehension of man's total physical and organic environment.

ERA	PERIOD	EPOCH	Ages of lower boundaries in millions of years
Cenozoic	Quaternary	Holocene	(12,000 years)
		Pleistocene	1.8
	Tertiary	Pliocene	5.0
		Miocene	22.5
		Oligocene	37.5
		Eocene	53.3
		Paleocene	65
Mesozoic	Cretaceous		136
	Jurassic		190-195
	Triassic		225
Paleozoic	Permian		280
	Pennsylvanian		320
	Mississippian		345
	Devonian		395
	Silurian		430-440
	Ordovician		500
	Cambrian		570
Pre-cambrian	Oldest evidence of life		2000
	Oldest dated rocks on earth		3700
	Probable age of earth		4700

The geologic time scale, with ages of the time division in millions of years (1972 radiometric data). Many of the dates are still approximate. Note that the rocks in the Gorge are all Cenozoic, which is only 11 percent of the time since life appeared, and less than 2 percent of the age of the earth.

Geologic Words and Symbols

The vocabulary of geology, having been coined to give accurate and concise abbreviations for complicated ideas, can sometimes intimidate the lay reader. *The Glossary of Geology,* published by the Geological Society of America, contains over 33,000 technical terms! However, fewer than 100 such terms will be used here. The first time they are used they will be given in *italics* and defined. If you read this section thoroughly before taking one of the trips, and particularly if you study the figures and diagrams, you should have no trouble.

Geologic words used in this book can be divided into six categories; those used for *geologic time;* for *rock assemblages,* for *rocks* themselves; for the *architecture* of the earth's crust; for *landforms;* and for *fossils.*

Terms used for geologic time — These are the clock terms of geology. Instead of seconds, minutes, hours, days, months, years, and historical periods, geologists divide time into longer units such as Epochs, Periods and Eras.

The 23 time terms given in the table are all we need to identify roughly the age of any rock or fossil found anywhere on Earth. Since in the Columbia River Gorge no rocks older than the Eocene are encountered, we will need to use only the first 9 of the 23 terms.

Terms used for rock assemblages — A rock type or assemblage of rock types that is different enough from those near it (or above or below it) so that it can be easily recognized in the field and its areal extent shown on a map is known as a *Formation.* Each formation is named for a geographic feature in the locality where it was first observed and described. Sometimes a rock name is used instead of the word Formation, as in "*Yakima Basalt.*" Page 4 lists some formations that will be seen on the trips. They are arranged (like the time scale) in the order of their age, from youngest (at the top) to oldest (at the bottom). Such a column is known as the "Stratigraphic Column" for a particular area; another area would have a different column of formations.

Terms used for rocks — Rocks, being made up of one or more minerals, are classified by the kinds, size, and arrangement of the mineral particles in them, and also by the way in which they originate. Although one must be able to identify the minerals in order to assign a sure name to a rock, we need not expand on this subject here, since the names of the rocks will be given as they appear in the roadside outcrops or cliffs above. Rocks

Age	Unit, age and composition
HOLOCENE-	Alluvium, talus, active landslides and debris flows
	Portland Hills Silt: Mostly loess (wind blown dust)
PLEISTOCENE	Intracanyon basaltic lavas, cinder cones and volcaniclastic deposits: Examples — cinder cones and lava of Hood River valley, intracanyon lavas from Wind River and Little White Salmon River valleys, Mount Defiance and Underwood Mountain lavas, and major High Cascade strato-volcanoes, such as St. Helens, Hood and Adams.
PLEISTOCENE- ___1.8 my___	Widespread olivine basalt volcanism. Examples: Larch Mountain, Mt. Zion, Mt. Pleasant, White Salmon and Chamberlain Hill shield volcanoes, and numerous cones and shields of *Boring Lava* in the Portland area.
PLIOCENE	*Troutdale Formation:* Depositional fill in the ancestral Columbia River valley and the delta and fan in the Portland basin. In part lacustrine silts, capped by gravels and sands.
___ 5 my ___	*The Dalles Formation:* Chiefly stream deposited volcaniclastic rocks in The Dalles area.
MIOCENE	*Yakima Basalt* of the *Columbia River Basalt* Group: Flood basalts from eastern Oregon; thick flows, pillow basalts and glass shard tuffs.
___ 22.5 my ___	*Eagle Creek Formation:* Coarse cobble gravels (mud flow deposits) and other volcaniclastic rocks, mostly andesitic.
OLIGOCENE	*Ohanapecosh Formation:* Slightly metamorphosed lavas, breccias and other volcaniclastic rocks, chiefly of andesitic composition, but increasing in basalt towards the west.

A simplified "stratigraphic column" giving the age of the *formations* and other lavas and sediments which may be seen in the Columbia River Gorge. The rock terms used are defined by the classifications on pages 6 and 7. These very brief descriptions of the composition of each rock unit are expanded in a more detailed table on p. 68-71.

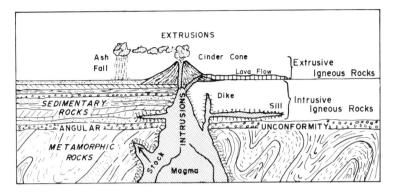

A hypothetical cross-section explaining the relationships between the three main types of rock (igneous, sedimentary and metamorphic) and the various terms used to identify some of the kinds of intrusive and extrusive igneous rock structures.

are classified into three major categories: *Igneous* ("fire formed") rocks which have cooled from a molten state; *Sedimentary* ("set down") rocks which have been formed from rock and soil particles which have been deposited or precipitated in basins by water, wind or ice and *Metamorphic* ("changed form") rocks which have been altered from their original state by the action of pressure, heat, and fluids, usually deep below the Earth's surface.

Igneous rocks are predominant in the Columbia River Gorge, and those types that appear there or nearby are classified in the table on page 6.

EXTRUSIVE igneous rocks include those which flowed out on the surface as lavas and *volcani-clastic* ("volcano-broken") rocks which blew into the air to fall as cinders and ash.

INTRUSIVE igneous rocks are those which cooled and solidified before they reached the surface.

SEDIMENTARY rocks (See page 7) are minor in amount in the Gorge but still important because they tell us much about what went on while they were being deposited. They also may contain fossils.

METAMORPHIC rocks are scarce, since they usually are formed deep below the surface, and the Gorge area is so young that deepseated rocks have not yet been exposed by erosion. The Ohanapecosh Formation, being the oldest and having been buried the deepest, is slightly metamorphosed.

ROCKNAMING MINERALS						
INTERPRETED LOCATION OF COOLING	SIZE AND ARRANGEMENT OF CRYSTAL GRAINS	QUARTZ				
		Present	Present	Present	Absent	Absent
		FELDSPAR				
		ORTHOCLASE (Potassium)		PLAGIOCLASE (High Sodium)		(High Calcium)
AIR FALL OR AIR FLOW (above surface)	VOLCANICLASTICS (Usually mostly glass)	ASH and TUFF (Usually Pumice and fine glass or crystal)			LAPILLI OR BOMBS Usually with Cinders (red and black)	
EXTRUSIVE (on or near the surface)	LAVAS & BRECCIAS (usually mostly microscopic grains)	RHYOLITE	DACITE		ANDESITE	BASALT DIABASE
EXTRUSIVE or Shallow intrusive	PORPHYRIES (some large grains in a finer-grained material)	Rocks listed both above and below may contain large crystals (frequently quartz or feldspar) in which case the prefix PORPHYRITIC or the suffix PORPHYRY is used.				
INTRUSIVE (Deep below the surface)	GRANITOID ROCKS (Coarse grains)	GRANITE (very rare in Cascades)	QUARTZ-DIORITE		DIORITE	GABBRO

A simplified classification of some of the igneous rocks that make up the Cascade Range. These rocks are mostly composed of the three minerals given at the top of the chart: *quartz, orthoclase* feldspar and *plagioclase* feldspar. The rock names are assigned on the basis of: a. the amount of glass (non-crystalline) in the rock, b. kind of mineral and its relative amount in the rock (%), c. the size of the mineral crystals, and the relative amounts of different size, d. the arrangement of the crystals in the rock. Light-colored rocks at the left become darker to the right in the table; fine-grained and glassy rocks at the top become coarser grained towards the bottom of the table. By far the most abundant rocks in the Cascade Range are the *basalts* and the *andesites*. Intrusive rocks are mostly *quartz-diorites*.

VOLCANICLASTIC		SIZE	SEDIMENTARY	
Sediments	Rocks		Sediments	Rocks
Ash	Fine tuff	Fine	Mud	Shale
Lapilli	Lapilli tuff	Medium	Sand	Sandstone
Blocks and bombs	Breccia	Coarse	Gravel	Conglomerate

A simplified size-classification of sedimentary and volcaniclastic rocks found in the Gorge. The fragmental rocks on the left were blown out of volcanoes; those on the right were ground up by water or ice during erosion. Both were deposited in layers, usually in lakes, rivers or shallow seas.

Terms used for structures – It is fortunate that much of the Earth's surface is covered with sedimentary rocks, and that changes in conditions during their deposition has resulted in an almost universal layering or bedding called *stratification*. Since these layers or beds were nearly all flat-lying when they were first deposited, appreciable divergence from a horizontal position tell us that the area has been tilted or folded. Any abrupt break in the lateral continuity of the layers suggests that the rocks have been displaced by movement along breaks or fractures known as *faults*. Folded and faulted structures are signs of mountain-making periods which are associated with uplift of the area. When uplift occurs, *erosion* or wearing away of the rocks produces gaps in the succession of layers (beds are

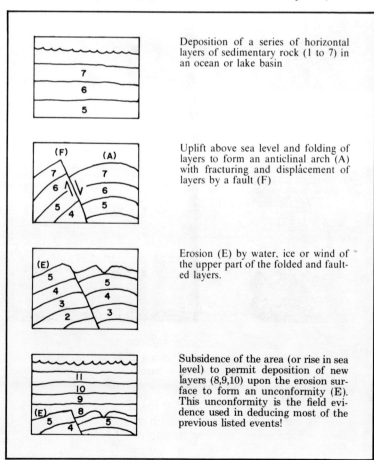

Deposition of a series of horizontal layers of sedimentary rock (1 to 7) in an ocean or lake basin

Uplift above sea level and folding of layers to form an anticlinal arch (A) with fracturing and displacement of layers by a fault (F)

Erosion (E) by water, ice or wind of the upper part of the folded and faulted layers.

Subsidence of the area (or rise in sea level) to permit deposition of new layers (8,9,10) upon the erosion surface to form an unconformity (E). This unconformity is the field evidence used in deducing most of the previous listed events!

Development of structures in layered rocks.

missing from the record). The structure representing this gap is called an *unconformity*. Many of the lines separating the Eras and Periods of the Time Chart were originally based on unconformities.

Igneous rocks also show distinctive structures which are valuable in the interpretation of past events. Lavas flow out in layers so layers can be traced. Secondly as lavas cool, they frequently contract and break into vertical columns. An individual basaltic lava flow can frequently be divided into an upper massive *entab-*

St. Peters Dome, an erosional remnant consisting of at least six flows of Yakima Basalt rising 1500 feet above the river south of Dodson (mile 36). (Historical Society Photo)

lature of hackly-jointed lava, and a lower *colonnade* of columnar-jointed basalt. Furthermore soil horizons formed originally at the earth's surface by weathering, may mark the contact between early and late flows, and suggest the passage of time between outpourings. If these horizons are no longer horizontal, or if the columns are no longer vertical, folding has taken place, and these folds can be mapped. Intrusive igneous rocks also have their structures, such as *dikes* (lava filling a fracture), and *sills* (lava spreading out between the layers of bedded sediments) and *stocks* (massive intrusions with a circular outline).

Terms used for landforms — Shapes of the surface of the land tell us much about underlying structures and the processes sculpturing the surface. Technical terms are used to specify these shapes. Since this story of the Columbia River Gorge is largely one of several kinds of volcanic activity, the terms used for volcanic forms become important. Of the six types of volcanoes illustrated on page 11, the first four appear in or near the Gorge.

Other landforms result from the processes of *erosion* or *deposition* by moving water, ice, or wind, or from *folding* (uparching or down warping) or *faulting* (movement along fractures in the crust).

A few examples found in the Gorge of each of these are:

Hanging valleys: valleys above the waterfalls in the gorge.

Cirques: rounded hollows carved by ice in the east rim of Benson Plateau.

Mesas: Table Mountain, flat-topped erosion remnant of a flat flow of Yakima Basalt.

Escarpments: East wall of Hood River valley, here produced by faulting.

Deltas: Alluvial deposit at the mouth of the Sandy River.

Incised meanders: Normal swinging loops of a river, that have been cut down (and frozen in place) as a result of the lowering of sea level. The Sandy River for the lower 20 miles of its course is the best example near the Gorge.

Terms used for fossils — Any identifiable remnant or evidence of past life found in the rocks is termed a *fossil.* In sedimentary rock assemblages each layer may contain fossils or assemblages of fossils representing life which existed only during the time those rocks were being deposited. Since the times of origin and extinction of these fossils is known from studies all over the earth, this means that we can use fossils to indicate the time when the formation itself was deposited.

Type	Characteristics	Examples	
1. Flood or plateau basalt	Very liquid lava; flows very widespread; emitted from fractures	Columbia River Plateau	One mile:
2. Shield volcano	Liquid lava emitted from a central vent; large; sometimes has a collapsed caldera	Larch Mtn., Sylvania, Highland Butte, Hawaiian volcanoes	
3. Cinder cone	Explosive liquid lava; small; emitted from a central vent; if continued long enough, may build up shield volcano	Mount Tabor, Mount Zion, Chamberlain Hill, Pilot Butte, Lava Butte	
4. Composite Volcano	More viscous lavas, much explosive (pyroclastic) debris; large; emitted from a central vent	Mount Hood, Mount St. Helens	
5. Plug dome	Very viscous lava; relativly small; can be explosive; commonly occurs adjacent to craters of composite volcanoes	Mount Lassen, Shastina, around Crater Lake, Mono Craters	
6. Caldera	Very large composite volcano collapsed after an explosive period; frequently associated with plug domes	Crater Lake, Newberry Caldera	

Types of volcanoes including examples and sketches. Note 1-mile-long scale bar in each diagram.

As might be expected, igneous rocks contain almost no fossils, and therefore fossils in the Gorge are restricted to petrified wood or leaves or casts of trees found in the soils formed between the lava flows or in the sedimentary interbeds between the sequence of lava flows, such as the Eagle Creek or Troutdale Formations. Even these formations are poor hosts for fossils, since they are non-marine and generally coarse-textured (largely conglomerates or breccias), whereas fossils are found most abundantly in fine grained marine sediments, which are entirely absent in the Gorge.

The study of fossils (*paleontology*) is so specialized that most geologists when mapping an area collect the fossils and send them to experts for identification and interpretation. This information enables a geologist to match up the formations in his area with those elsewhere, even though the rocks may not be similar. Furthermore, the life forms represented by the fossils can tell much about the landscape in which they lived, whether in the deep sea (fish), near the shoreline (oysters), or on dry land (horses).

Use of geologic symbols — putting it all on paper — Geologists are great believers in the maxim "one picture is worth a thousand words."

The most necessary and basic tool of the geologist is the map. It may only be a road map or a forest map; but preferably it is a topographic or "contour" map, upon which the elevations above sea level are shown by lines. The geologist in the field places geological information on these maps (page 55).

While a good topographic map is a basic tool of a geologist, the "geologic map" is most often his primary product. In order to put geologic information on the topographic map, the geologist has developed sets of abbreviated symbols and patterns to indicate rock formations, lines of contact between formations and structures (folds, faults and dikes, etc.).

The second most important product of the geologist is the *"stratigraphic column"* or time table (see page 4) which places the formations in their natural order, the oldest on the bottom and the youngest on top, and summarizes their time span, composition, thickness and fossil content.

A third geologic product is a *"geologic cross section"* which is a vertical slice through the sedimentary layer-cake which lies beneath a topographic profile of the surface elevations, and shows the geologist's interpretation of what goes on deep underground.

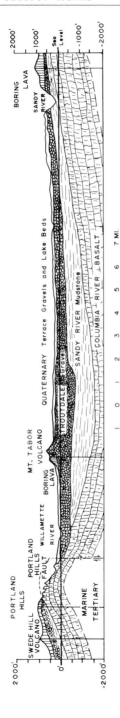

Geologic cross-section through the Portland area (after Trimble, 1963). Taken on an east-west line from west of Sylvan to east of Troutdale. The Yakima Basalt has been folded and faulted to produce the Portland Hills anticline and the Portland synclinal basin, which was filled with Sandy River mudstone and Troutdale gravel and then intruded by Boring volcanoes at Swede Hill, Mount Tabor and Chamberlain Hill east of Troutdale. Note that vertical scale is over five times the horizontal scale.

Geologic principles and processes

Plate tectonics — the new geology — Since the early 1960's, a scientific revolution has upset our 100-year-old ideas about the permanency of the continents; ocean basins; the origin of mountains; and volcanic activity. We now believe that the earth's crust is divided into seven large (and several smaller) rigid plates, which move separately. The Atlantic Ocean was formed, beginning about 200 million years ago, by the splitting off of the North and South American plates from the European and African plates. The widening gap was filled, as the plates moved apart at a rate of a few inches per year, by sub-oceanic basalt and gabbro dikes rising along the central fissure which now appears as the mid-Atlantic Ridge.

If the Atlantic Ocean becomes wider, then the Pacific Ocean must become narrower, and indeed, most of the Pacific is bordered by deep trenches where the heavier oceanic crust of the Pacific plate has plunged downward to slide beneath the lighter and higher-floating continental plates. This *"subduction"* of the oceanic crust carries with it ocean bottom sediment and contained water on top of the plunging plate, which melt to produce magma and igneous activity within the overlying continental plate. This is an over simplification of why the Pacific Ocean is ringed with volcanoes, the "Circle of Fire", and with mountains subject to earthquakes.

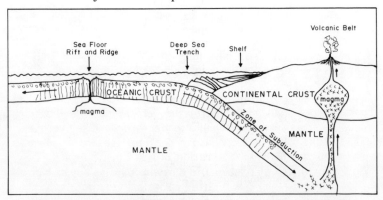

Plate tectonics. Volcanic belts, such as the Cascade Range, result from the oceanic crust, with its contained water, being shoved down (*subducted*) beneath the edge of the continent, to a depth where it will melt to produce liquid rock (*magma*). The magma then works its way to the surface to form volcanoes and lavas. This movement of the oceanic crust begins at the rift and ridge in both the Pacific and Atlantic Oceans, which are filled in and built up by submarine volcanism where the ocean floor pulls apart.

Internal and external geologic processes — The theory of plate tectonics helps explain the internal causes and location of *magma* within the crust, and the resulting *volcanism* when that magma comes to the surface. It helps explain the origin and location of *folding, faulting* and *uplift* of mountains. It also

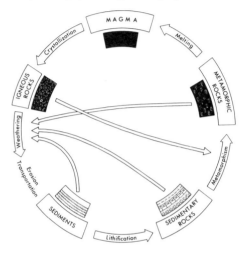

The rock cycle, shown diagramatically. If uninterrupted, the cycle will continue completely around the outer margin of the diagram from magma through igneous rocks, sediments, sedimentary rocks, metamorphic rocks, and back again to magma. The cycle may be interrupted, however, at various points along its course and follow the path of one of the arrows crossing through the interior of the diagram.

follows that when mountains are uplifted or built by volcanism, the surface processes of *weathering, erosion, transportation* (mostly by gravity and water), and *deposition* of sedimentary rocks can take place. Rocks also can be changed by such internal processes as *lithification* (alteration of a sediment to a rock by compaction and cementation), *metamorphism* by deep burial and heating, and even by melting to form a new magma.

We have already seen that the geologic process of volcanism was the dominating theme during nearly all of the 40 or 50 million years recorded in the rocks of the Columbia River Gorge. Literally hundreds of volcanic vents of all types have been active in or within a few miles of the present Gorge. Volcanic explosions have built up thick layers of ash and breccia; lava from volcanic fissures and mudflows from volcanic slopes have repeatedly filled the ancestral valley and are now exposed in the present walls.

One internal process of great interest to westerners is seismicity, or earthquake activity. Oregon lies just east of the boundary of the North American and Pacific plates, in the circum-Pacific earthquake belt, where 80 percent of all earthquakes occur.

Geologists believe that most earthquakes are produced by sudden relief of stresses which have gradually accumulated beneath the surface due to slow movements of the crustal plates of the earth. When these stresses finally exceed the strength of the rocks, they break or slip along planes of weakness known as *faults*. This sudden slip or break shakes the earth.

Displacement of the rocks seen along fault lines therefore tells us that earthquakes occurred there in the past. It is also believed that the longer a fault line is, and the greater the amount of movement there has been, the more chance there is for earthquakes to occur in the future, and the greater those earthquakes may be.

For reasons still unknown to geologists or geophysicists, major earthquakes (magnitude 7 or more) have not occurred in historic time within the area of the lower Columbia River. California to the south and the Puget Sound area to the north has been much more active. They suspect that when we learn more about the configuration of the plate junctions in the northwest we may come up with an answer.

Folding and crumpling of the rock layers is another internal process. The jostling of the plates against each other produces lateral stresses which bow up the crust into *anticlines* and down into *synclines*. The main arch of the Cascades is one such uplift, even better examples are the Portland Hills anticline, the Portland-Vancouver and Tualatin basins, and the splendid set of folds so well exposed between Hood River and The Dalles.

External geologic processes are also effective in producing landscape features. *Weathering* breaks down solid rocks and produces soils which are then removed by gravity (talus deposits, landslides). *Erosion* by streams then acts as a conveyor-belt to carry away these loosened materials and eventually transport them to the ocean where they form new sedimentary deposits. As will be seen, the powerful Columbia River has for at least 20 million years repeatedly recut its canyon; it has maintained a course through the Cascades to the sea in spite of obstructions of uplift, folding, faulting, lava flows and landslides.

Reconstructing the past — Geologists take all the observations on the distribution of rock types, formations, structures and fossils in a given area and fit them together so that they can be interpreted to tell the story of the consecutive events that make up the history of the area's geologic past.

The basic guidelines for such interpretations may be summarized in a few simple laws:

1. Layers that are not horizontal today, have been tilted or folded since they were deposited (*Law of Original Horizontality*).
2. Layers lying on top of other layers are younger (were deposited later) than those beneath (*Law of Superposition*).
3. Igneous rocks intruded into other rocks are younger than the rocks they intrude. (*Law of Cross-Cutting Relationships*).
4. Progressively more complicated animals appear as fossils later in the record than the more simple forms of life (*Law of Evolution*).

Although deductions can best be made about environment and origin from sedimentary rocks or the fossils contained within them, igneous rocks, so abundant in the Columbia River Gorge, can also tell us a great deal about the past. Lava flows, ash falls and mud flows are layered too, although not as evenly as are marine sediments. Lava and ash can also be more easily dated by radioactive methods than can sediments.

The evidence and logic used in the interpretations advanced in the following pages cannot be given in full, but enough is given, it is hoped, to guide the interested reader to the more complete accounts in the reports listed in the bibliography at the end of the book. The reader is further cautioned that the account set forth here is an integrated "moving picture" resulting from gathering together many hypothesis by many workers from many thousands of observations made over a hundred years.

This history, for the area of the Columbia River Gorge, is summarized, first, in the stratigraphic column on page 4 and then by the following short condensed summary of the chief events of the geologic history. We will later discuss in Chapter 3 the more detailed sequence of events during the last 40 million years.

Summary of events

Paleocene and Eocene — 28 million year interval from 65 to 37 my ago.

The Cretaceous seas have just retreated, once and for all, from eastern Oregon, and the shoreline is now near the western edge of the present Cascade Range, bordered by a broad coastal plain supporting coal forests. Submarine volcanoes and volcanic islands occupy the present site of the Coast Range, and a line of explosive volcanoes east of the present Willamette Valley

is piling up thousands of feet of volcanic products. Volcanoes
are also widespread in eastern Oregon. The climate is subtropi-
cal. Plants include palms, figs, avocados. Four-toed horses,
rhinos, tapirs and crocodiles occupy the forests and swamps.

Oligocene and Lower Miocene — 20 my interval from 37 to
17 my ago.

The exposive activity of the western Cascade volcanoes continues, lakes become ash-filled in eastern Oregon, and shorelines
are built westward into the shallowing seas. Cascade volcanoes
are still too low to affect the universal warm temperate climate.
Plants include magnolia and sequoia; three-toed horses,
camels, giant pigs, small saber-tooth cats, oreodonts and giant
archaic titanotheres occupy the landscape.

Middle Miocene to Lower Pliocene — 13 my interval from 17
to 4 my ago.

Great basalt floods pour out repeatedly during a period of
7 my, covering more than 50,000 square miles of the northwest.
Originating in dike-swarms in central and eastern Oregon and
Washington, they pour westward to the sea down the broad
ancestral Columbia River valley, which is repeatedly displaced
to the north and west around the edge of the flows. Warping
of this great monotonous lava plain forms basins which become
filled with silt and gravel from the river and volcanoclastics
from a new swarm of low Cascade volcanoes and cinder cones
which, except for the Portland area, lie east of the old extinct
volcanic chain. The High Cascades begin to fold up into a great
arch (as does the Coast Range to the west) forcing the sea westward to near the present coastline. The rising mountain barrier
produces a dryer climate east of the Cascades. The climate is
cooling everywhere, and plants similar to today's are appearing.
The horse changes from three-toed to one-toed as forests give
way to grassy plains; the archaic giant mammals disappear, and
are replaced by rhinos, camels, antelope, bear, mammoths and
mastodons.

Middle Pliocene to Present — the last 4 my.

Many of the great High Cascade stratovolcanoes begin to
build, and hundreds of smaller shields and cinder cones begin
to dot the landscape. Several of these latter were located in
the valleys tributary to the Columbia so that their lavas flow
down into the canyon to repeatedly dam the river and form
temporary lakes.

Ice sheets from Canada repeatedly advance into northern Washington and retreat with accompanying changes in sea level and climate. The increased precipitation accelerates erosion of the Gorge, so that the river is able to maintain its course in spite of the continuing rise of the Cascade arch. Numerous small glaciers appear above elevations of 3000 feet, and major glaciers scar the flanks of the giant volcanoes and extend many miles down adjacent valleys. Wind-blown dust (*loess*) from the glacial mills to the north mantle the lower landscapes.

A series of catastrophic floods in the latest Pleistocene strip the soil and loess from the Gorge walls up to elevations of 1000 feet, and broaden the valley bottom with the formation of many water falls. This oversteepening of the valley walls results in numerous landslides, especially in the softer old rocks on the north side. One slide temporarily dams the river as late as 1260 A.D., and probably gave rise to the legend of the Bridge of the Gods. Sea level rises 350 feet at the end of the ice age.

Man appeared in North America at least 35,000 years ago, and first occupied the Gorge at least 12,000 years ago, where he lived mostly off the fish, taken near rapids. He may well also have contributed to the extinction during the last 10,000 years of the large herbivore mammals such as the mammoth, mastodon, horse, camel and many others. The history of man in the Gorge is summarized on p. 59-65.

CHAPTER 2
THE NATURAL SETTING

"There's nothing constant in the universe, All ebb
and flow, and every shape that's born bears in its
womb the seeds of change."

Ovid, *Metamorphosis, XV* (56-117 AD)

The river

The Columbia River drains an area nearly as large as Texas.
Rainfall in the headwaters and tributaries is so great that it
carries the second largest volume of water in the United States
(after the Mississippi). It is the largest river in the Western
Hemisphere to enter the Pacific Ocean, and occupies the only
northwest valley which provides ready access to the continental
interior.

Length of the Columbia River (7th longest in the United States)	1243 miles
Area drained by the Columbia River	259,000 square miles
Average discharge (2nd largest in U.S.)	194,600 cubic feet per second
Maximum recorded discharge (1894)	1,240,000 cubic feet per second
Minimum recorded discharge (1937)	37,000 cubic feet per second
Average width of river	1 mile
Average width of valley (rim to rim)	3 miles
Length of Gorge (Troutdale-Dalles)	75 miles
Average height of walls (south side)	1500-3000 feet
Maximum elevation of walls (Benson Plateau)	4000 feet
(Mt. Defiance)	4960 feet
(Table Mt.)	3400 feet

Some statistics on the Columbia River and Gorge.

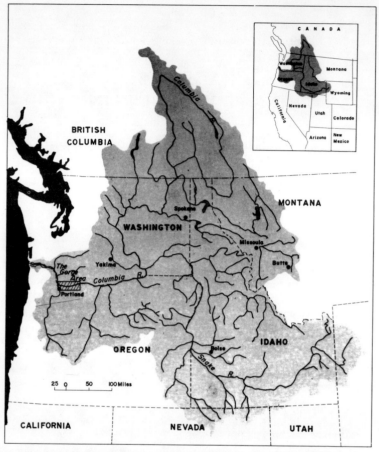

The Columbia River and its tributaries drain more than a
quarter of a million square miles of Oregon, Washington,
Idaho, Montana and British Columbia (plus small areas of
Wyoming, Nevada and Utah). While the Columbia itself is
over 1200 miles long, its largest tributary, the Snake, is over
1000 miles long.

The river drops nearly 1300 feet from near the Canadian
border, so that eleven dams can generate power from the main
stem flow. More than 160 other dams exist or are being con-
structed on tributaries in four states and Canada. Within the
Gorge, at Bonneville and The Dalles, dams have raised the
average water level from 25 feet abve sea level near Portland
to 72 feet behind the dam at Bonneville and 160 feet at The
Dalles.

The range

The volcano-crowned Cascade Range,* completely breached by the Columbia River Gorge, is the dominant mountain range of the Pacific Northwest.

Nowhere in North America, except perhaps in the Aleutian Islands, is there such a concentration and such a variety of volcanoes as in the Cascades. Extending from beyond Mount Baker on the north to Mount Lassen in California on the south, this 600-mile-long chain of Plio-Pleistocene and Recent volcanoes exhibit a great variety of types of volcanic activity, ranging from *cinder cones* and *shield volcanoes,* through *compound* and *composite* volcanoes to *plug domes* and *calderas* (See page 11). Fourteen of the nearly one thousand volcanoes in the Cascade Range rise to elevations above 9,000 feet. From north to south, they are:

Washington:

Mount Baker	10,750
Glacier Peak	10,436
Mount Rainier	14,410
Mount Adams	12,307
Mount St. Helens	9,671

Oregon:

Mount Hood	11,245
Mount Jefferson	10,495
North Sister	10,094
Middle Sister	10,053
South Sister	10,354
Mount Mazama (Crater Lake)	14,000?
Mount Pitt (McLoughlin)	9,510

California:

Mount Shasta	14,162
Mount Lassen	10,457

In Oregon, these high peaks rest upon and among lower shield volcanoes which were built up by more fluid basaltic and andesitic lava mostly during the Pliocene epoch, derived from a zone

---

*The Cascade Range was named from the "mountains by the Cascades" of the Columbia River, that hazardous barrier to river transport eliminated only by completion of the canal and locks in 1886.

of deep-seated north-south fissures which lie, as a general rule, east of the crest of the older Cascades which is Miocene or older. In many cases they were built up in valleys cut in the older lavas. Since some of these valleys have been glaciated, we know that the volcanoes were active during the Pleistocene and Holocene.

In Washington, the Ice Age peaks usually rest directly upon lower Tertiary lavas and even, in the case of Mount Baker and Glacier Peak in the northern Cascades, upon the pre-Tertiary metamorphic terrain.

In addition to the composite high peaks and shield volcanoes, we find cinder cones in abundance. Basaltic lavas from hundreds of these cones have within the last few tens to hundreds of thousands years flowed down many of the valleys tributary to the Columbia River Gorge.

The lava shields and towering glaciated peaks of the Cascade Range now separate the well-watered tree-covered western part of Oregon and Washington from the arid or semi-arid eastern plateaus and basins. They form a nearly continuous, dominantly volcanic (except for northern Washington) mountain barrier 600 miles long and 30 to 70 miles wide, with relatively few passes less than 4000 feet in elevation.

The Gorge

The Columbia River has carved a spectacular 75-mile-long canyon through an upland surface (best developed south of the gorge) which is a broad arch rising 133 feet per mile from near Troutdale to 4000 feet at its crest near Benson Plateau, and then dropping steeply towards Hood River. This surface is surmounted by several volcanic shields such as Larch Mountain and Mount Defiance which rise another thousand feet or more. The upland surface south of the Gorge is deeply dissected by 11 narrow V-shaped canyons; of these, only Eagle Creek canyon is more than 10 miles long.

Possibly the greatest concentration of high waterfalls in North America appear on the south walls of the Gorge, mostly near the mouths of these side canyons. Twenty five falls are well enough known to be mapped, and 11 over 100 feet high can be seen from the freeway or scenic highway. Another 13 lie from 2 to 7 miles up the canyons. Many of these falls occur in the center of alcoves or amphitheatres much wider than the falls themselves. How these alcoves occurred is an interesting problem that will be discussed later.

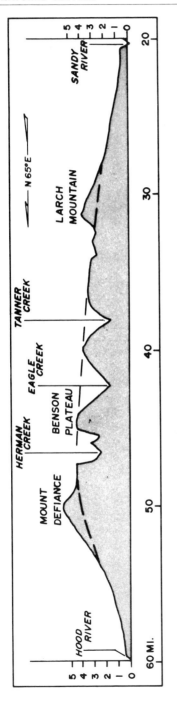

Profile from Sandy River to Hood River, drawn 5 miles south of the Gorge, to show the arching of the Cascades which took place during the last 10 million years. Less than 1000 feet of this arch can be attributed to volcanic buildup. Mileage from Portland, elevations in thousands of feet.

Mileage	Name of Falls	(Creek)	Height in ft.	Comments
22.9	Unnamed		?	Thin fall beneath Crown Point
23.9	*Latourelle		250	Talbot State Park
25.5	*Shepperds Dell	(Young)	?	State Park
26.0	*Bridal Veil		?	Below scenic highway
26.9	Coopey		117	
28.8	Mist		?	High above on cliff
29.0	*Wahkeena, lower and upper		242	Main falls upstream
29.5	*Multnomah, lower		69	Total fall 620
	upper		551	
	Middle falls		60	In first two miles up
	Upper falls		75	Multnomah Creek
31.8	Oneonta		100	Up gorge 900 feet
32.0	*Horsetail		208 (221?)	
36.0	*Elowah	(McCord)	289	800' south of highway
37.2	Moffett			1000' up canyon
38.3	Wahclella	(Tanner)	125	2 miles upstream
39.8	Eagle Creek: 7 falls			
	Metlako			2.0 miles upstream
	(Campgrounds Punch Bowl			2.5 miles upstream
	located at Loowit			4.0 miles upstream
	4.5, 5.3 & Unnamed			4.2 miles upstream
	7.5 miles Unnamed			5.5 miles upstream
	upstream) Tunnel			6.5 miles upstream
	Unnamed			7.0 miles upstream
43.0	Dry		?	2 miles by road
52.0	Lindsey		104	State Park
52.5	Warren		200	
53.0	*Starvation		186	State Park

Better known falls in the Columbia River Gorge. Mileages given are on the freeway, but falls are best seen from the scenic highway. *Marks those that are the most accessible.

Side of river	Name	Approx. elev. in ft.	Comments
S	Rocky Butte	600	Remnant of a Pliocene volcano
S	Rooster Rock	200	Basalt landslide block
S	St. Peter's Dome	1500	Pinnacle of Yakima Basalt flows
N	Beacon Rock	850	Volcanic neck or dike of probable volcano
N	Aldrich Butte	1000	Erosion remnant of Eagle Creek Formation
S	Tooth Rock	350	Landslide block of Yakima Basalt
N	Wind Mountain	1900	Intrusive stock of possible Pliocene volcano
S	Shellrock Mountain	2100	Intrusive stock of possible Pliocene volcano
S	Mitchell Point	1150	Tilted block of Yakima Basalt and Troutdale Formation

Isolated pinnacles and promontories in the Columbia River gorge and their height and origin.

Isolated pinnacles and promontories, the favorite and perilous haunts of rock climbers, punctuate the landscape every few miles. The most spectacular of these was named Beacon Rock by Lewis and Clark in 1806. It is a vertical-walled pinnacle 850 feet high. Another 200 feet high pinnacle named Rooster Rock occurs below Crown Point on the south shore. It was given a more earthy, phallic name by pioneers! Wind and Shellrock Mountains are the highest of all, rising 2000 feet on either side of the river and have aptly been titled "Twin Guardians of the Columbia." Mitchell Point, 4 miles west of Hood River, once rose so steeply from the water's edge that the original scenic highway tunneled through it, with windows cut along the cliff face. Tooth Rock at Bonneville had also to be penetrated by tunnels and by-passed by a bridge.

The north side of the valley does not present the almost continuous cliffs of the south, it is less steep, very little of the upland surface remains, and cliffs that do appear are usually landslide-produced, and farther from the river. Of the central 25 miles of the north shore between Cape Horn and Dog Mountain, 16 miles, or 65 percent, has been greatly modified by landsliding, some of which extends back more than 4 miles north of the river. The total area affected by landslides in the gorge is over 50 square miles, of which about 5 square miles is now actively moving each year.

Few waterfalls appear north of the Columbia River, partially as a result of the landsliding and partially because the Columbia River Basalt, the chief cliff-and-waterfall-maker, covers only relatively small areas north of the Columbia. Four rivers enter from the north, the Washougal, Wind, Little White Salmon, White Salmon, and Klickitat, whereas only two rivers, Sandy and Hood, enter from the south.

The weather

Average annual rain and snowfall at east Portland (airport) is 42 inches; this average increases rapidly eastward to over 100 inches at Wind River and 150 inches in the Bull Run area, immediately south of the Gorge; then it drops rather abruptly to 29 and 14 inches at Hood River and The Dalles respectively. Fall and winter precipitation accounts for 70 to 80 percent; springs and summers are relatively dry. Every few years, freezing winter rain (locally called "silver thaw") can make the highways in the Gorge almost impassable.

Temperatures seldom go below freezing for more than a few days, but when they do, the freezing spray from the waterfalls make unusually spectacular ice displays. A particularly hard freeze in 1964 produced so much ice below Multnomah Falls

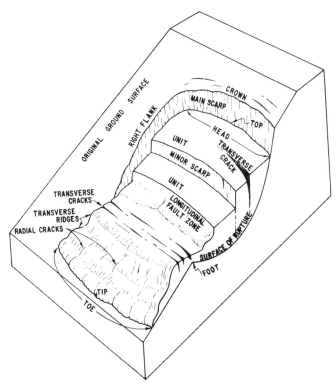

Some characteristics of landslides. The schematic diagram shows the progressive headward development of multiple arcuate slip-surfaces, the hummocky nature of the toe portion of the slide, the tilting of trees and the formation of depressed areas which may be occupied by small lakes. See also maps on pages 54 and 55. Illustration from *California Geology.* May, 1974.

that a miniature glacier over 500 feet long and 30 feet thick moved down the canyon below the falls and broke the abutments of the highway bridge east of the lodge. During the colder climate late in the last century the entire river froze over many times.

The trails

Although this is primarily a highway guide, no geologist could fail to mention the many forest trails which extend both north and south from the gorge to falls, lakes and viewpoints. Over 120 miles of trails on the south side of the central gorge (MP

26 to 53) are logged and detailed on the "Forest Trails Map" published by the Mount Hood National Forest. A more elaborate guide, which inclues map and trails north of the Gorge as well, is in "The Columbia River Gorge — An Enjoyment Guide" by Jack Grauer.

The vegetation

To those interested in the wealth and variety of Oregon's native plants, the scenic highway trip offers enough tantalizing "Do not touch" displays of colorful species to make investigating the flora on side trails and hiking trips very attractive. A guidebook to western plants (there are several good ones) is a necessity for real study, but even the geologist author must remark on the great variety that appears in the mile or so of the Scenic Highway switchbacks just east of Crown Point. In this sheltered landslide cove, logged off soon after the turn of the century, the climax Douglas fir forest has not yet driven out the understory of alder, western red cedar, western hemlock, yew, and both big-leaf and vine maple. Brush and shrub during different times of the year include ferns (sword, bracken, five finger, maiden-hair, deer), berries (elder, salmon, thimble, snow, black, and wood huckleberry), false solomon seal, skunk cabbage, devils club, oxalis and, in the moss on trees, licorice fern.

This western Oregon second-growth rain-forest assemblage gives way to a semi-arid forest as one enters the Hood River Valley and proceeds eastward towards The Dalles. Oak and yellow pine rapidly replace fir and hemlock within a few miles.

CHAPTER 3
GEOLOGIC HISTORY OF THE GORGE

"The traveler who is curious; who sees only the
depth and width and length of the Gorge and
neglects its fourth dimension, which is time; who is
content with the Gorge as a still picture, and fails
to recognize that the present scene is only one
changing frame of a moving picture, the earlier
frames of which can be equally vivid; who does not
see, in the daily toll of mud and sand washed
seaward by the river, the certainty that the walls
of the Gorge must become less and less steep until
the whole rugged range is reduced to faint slopes
near sea level; this traveler has seen the Gorge
only with his eyes, not with his mind."

(Mackin & Cary, 1965)

The ancient framework (before 50 my ago)
Geologists and astronomers tell us that the earth and solar
system was formed about 5 billion years ago; that the oldest
rocks so far found on earth are less than 4 billion years old;
and that the history of the earth is fairly well known only during
the last half billion years.

Interpretation of the early pre-history of the Pacific Northwest relies on information derived from the areas of older folded
and altered rocks located in northern Washington, eastern Oregon and Idaho and southwestern Oregon. These rocks are mostly from 100 million to a quarter billion (250 million) years old.

The Columbia River Gorge is located in the center of a broad
triangle, composed almost entirely of rocks less than 50 million
years old. Any specific statements about the older history are
pure conjectures. We can make a few general statements, however.

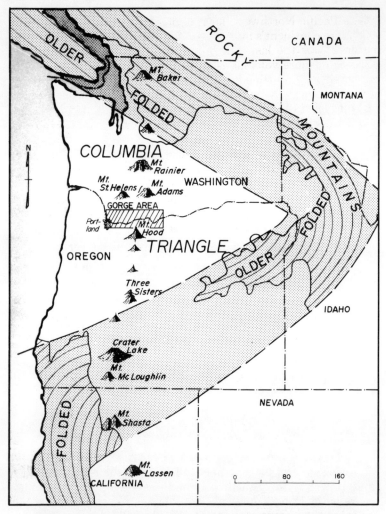

The Columbia Triangle of the Pacific Northwest. The older
(lined) rocks (Mesozoic and Paleozoic) in the northwest are
highly folded, metamorphosed and intruded. Later (Cenozoic)
rocks in the center of the map are much less disturbed. The
trend of the folding in the older rocks in southern Oregon
is to the northeast, beneath the Cascades into north-eastern
Oregon, where this trend bends sharply to the left in the Wallowa Mountains, and presumably continues into northwestern Washington. This "kink" in the Mesozoic mountain
chain is thought to have been formed by shearing and rotat-
ing stresses on a large scale during the Cretaceous and lower
Tertiary.

The Pacific Northwest, located near the western edge of the American continent's moving crustal plate, has been "where the action is" for the last half billion years. Arcs of Permian and Triassic offshore volcanic islands (like the Aleutians of today) may well have outlined the Columbia triangle only to be destroyed during a Mesozoic period of subduction and mountain making. The last sea to enter eastern Oregon (in the Cretaceous) was filled with gravels, sands and muds eroded from this mountain arc.

The dawn of modern life
(Eocene — 53.5 to 37.5 my)

By the beginning of Tertiary time the shallow (Cretaceous) sea, which had for many million years covered much of Oregon, was gone forever from the eastern part of the Pacific Northwest,

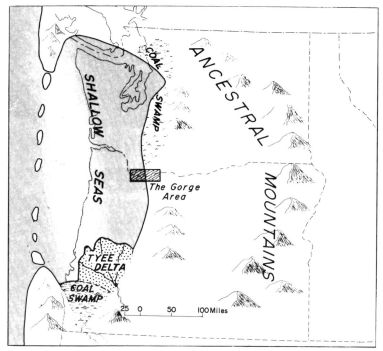

Eocene geography of the northwest. This is one interpretation of the 40 my old landscape. A broad embayment is partly cut off from the sea by offshore volcanic islands; a great river delta and adjacent coal swamps rim the embayment, while it is being filled in with ash from volcanoes to the east, and debris from the higher mountains still farther east.

and in the Columbia Triangle the sea consisted of a partially enclosed marine embayment restricted to western Oregon and Washington. The shoreline was near or just east of the present western edge of the Cascade Range. The sea was dotted with basaltic island volcanoes, and bordered by low plains covered with tropical coal swamps. Great deltas at the mouths of large rivers built out into the shallow seas. The eastern part of the Columbia Triangle was occupied by explosive volcanoes which were beginning to build up there and along the present Cascades, adding materials to the sea and slowly forcing the shoreline westward. Palms, figs and avocados flourished; this was the beginning of the age of mammals, and primitive four-toed horses, archaic titanotheres, rhinoceroses, tapirs and crocodiles inhabited the rivers and plains.

Continuation of early volcanism
(Oligocene — 37.5 to 22.5 my)

The 15 million years of Oligocene time was a continuation and expansion throughout the Cascade area and in central Oregon, of volcanic activity that eventually built up a 3 mile thick pile of varicolored volcanic ash and mud and lava flows both north and south of the present Columbia River Gorge *(Ohanapecosh Formation* and *Little Butte Series)* and in central Oregon *(Clarno Formation)*. The shallowing sea by now had retreated still farther to the west, and was dotted with large islands. Towards the end of the Oligocene, a series of cataclysmic volcanic explosions, perhaps similar to but much greater than the Mount Mazama-Crater Lake event, threw out a mile thick series of thick pumice ash *(Stevens Ridge Formation)* which may also have fallen and been washed into central Oregon lakes *(John Day Formation)*.

During uppermost Oligocene time, there was a period of relative quiet, in which deep weathering resulting from the still rather tropical climate produced a 30 to 50-foot thick red soil (saprolite) which can be seen in the Gorge above the town of Stevenson.

The tropical climate, was beginning to change to a still warm but more temperate one, with liquidamber, magnolia, dawn redwood (metasequoia) trees becoming common; three-toed horses, camels, giant pigs, small sabre-tooth cats and oreodonts ("pigdogs") roamed the plains in eastern Oregon.

The great basalt floods
(Miocene — 22.5 to 5.0 my)

Local basins in the Gorge area continued in lower Miocene time to fill with volcanic gravels, tuffs, and mud-flow breccias

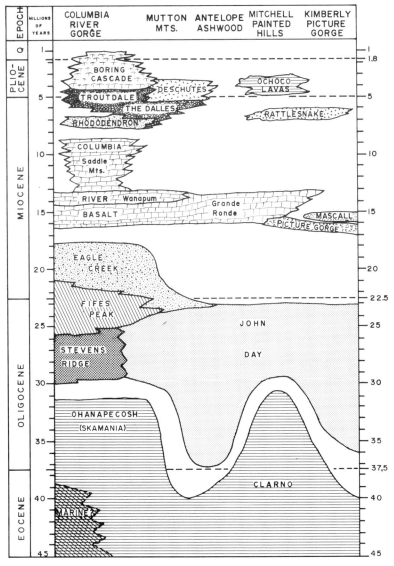

Tertiary time and rocks from the Columbia River Gorge to
Central Oregon. Note that on the vertical scale, the span
of time is proportional to distance; as a result, the last 5
million years (Miocene to the Present) is too compressed to
show any details, these are expanded later on page 43. Also
note that the east-west geographic extent of the rocks units
is shown by their spread from right to left (in part after
Woodburne, 1977).

(Eagle Creek Formation). Forests grew up, only to be over-whelmed by new mud flows from nearby volcanoes. In central Oregon, continuing volcanic activity in the form of ash falls and flows of incandescent pumice added to the lake deposits *(John Day Formation)*.

Middle Miocene, and more specifically the period from about 17 to 10 million years ago, was the time of the greatest lava outpouring ever to occur in North America. The lavas of the *Columbia River Basalt Group* which form most of the great black cliffs in the Gorge were formed during this period of only 7 million years. This flood was the latest (but not the greatest) of at least seven similar great outpourings of basalt which occurred on other continents, widely dispersed in time and space.

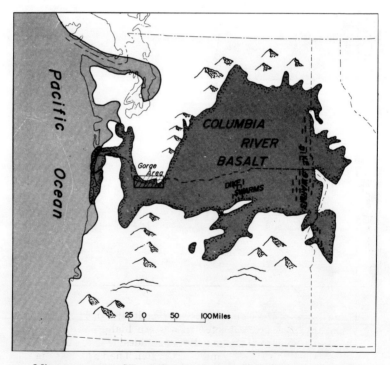

Miocene geography of the northwest. This 20 my old land-scape was dominated for more than 8 my by outpourings of thousands of cubic miles of the Columbia River Basalt, most-ly from north-south trending fissures along the eastern border of present-day Oregon and Washington. The flows eventually covered over 50 thousand square miles to a depth of up to a mile, and poured westward down the ancestral Columbia River valley to the sea.

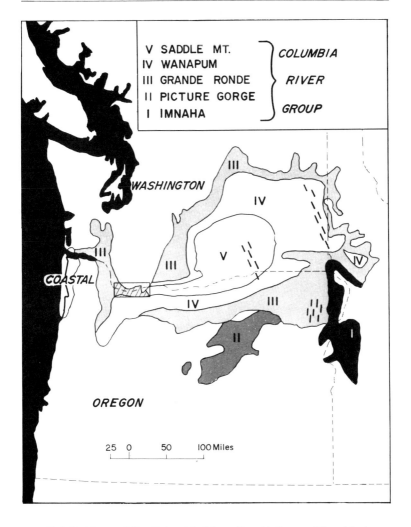

V   SADDLE MT.
IV WANAPUM   COLUMBIA
III GRANDE RONDE   RIVER
II PICTURE GORGE
I   IMNAHA   GROUP

Subdivisions of the Columbia River Basalt Group. The oldest
(*Imnaha*) flows are restricted to western Idaho and the extreme eastern edge of Oregon. The next oldest (*Picture Gorge*)
occupy the John Day Country in Oregon. The last three are
collectively known as the *Yakima Basalt*. The *Grande Ronde*
flows of the Yakima Basalt cover the largest area of all, and
reached the sea near Astoria. As the Columbia River basin
sank, the *Wanapum* flows were less extensive, and the last
Saddle Mountain flows can be found down river only as far
as Mosier. Basalts of similar age along the northern coast
of Oregon may have erupted from separate vents or may be
extensions of the flows from the east.

In the northwest, movements of the continental plate pulled the crust apart, and far to the east of the Gorge hundreds of mostly north-south trending fissures allowed the magma from deep within or below the crust to pour out on the surface. Several areas of *"dike swarms"* (clusters of lava-filled fissures) are known in the Columbia Basin, the largest are in the Wallowa Mountains of northeastern Oregon and along the Idaho border; others occur north of John Day, Oregon and Pasco, Washington.

The basalt flowed hundreds of miles westward from the swarms of dikes in these eastern sources, spreading out as they filled the valleys to eventually cover most of the Columbia Triangle east of the line of ancestral Cascade volcanoes. The lava floods which came through the Cascades (somewhat south of the present Gorge) and continued westward into the Miocene sea near Astoria are the first evidence of an ancient Columbia River valley.

The successive outpourings of Columbia River Basalt Group are divided into five episodes. The earliest began along the Oregon-Idaho border *(Imnaha),* followed by those in central Oregon *(Picture Gorge).* The Yakima Basalt, the most widespread flood of all, begins with flows *(Grande Ronde)* which seem to have originated in the Wallowa Mountain region, and flowed westward all the way to the sea. Later outpourings *(Wanapum* and *Saddle Mountain)* covered smaller areas in the basin, but also came down the Columbia valley into western Oregon, each time shoving the river in the Gorge area farther to the north.

During the later episodes, sediments from the ancestral Columbia and other rivers coming into the interior basin became interbedded within the flows (*Ellensberg Formation,* etc.) and filled local basins over much of the Columbia triangle.

The progressive restriction of the later flows to the center of the Columbia Triangle suggests that downwarping of the basin began soon after the early outpourings; certainly folding around the edges of the basin and farther west in the Portland and Tualatin areas also commenced before the last basalt floods. The Columbia River, now well established in the "Big Bend" around the north and west edge of the Columbia Basin, was able to cut down through most of the folds as they rose; the Columbia Hills-Rattlesnake Hills fold, however, diverted it east to the Wallula Gateway.

About 12 million years ago, deep seated quartz-diorite intrusions penetrated the older basalt flows and cooled below the surface to form the massive Wind Mountain and Shell Rock Mountain stocks, and the smaller Government Island group of intrusions to the west. The Laurel Hill intrusion south of Mount Hood came in at about the same time. It is not known whether these intrusions ever reached the surface to form volcanoes.

Late in the Miocene, a relatively short period of renewed explosive volcanism in the Cascades spread a local blanket of ash, cinders and debris from andesitic vents *(Rhododendron Formation)*, covering much of the surface of the Yakima Basalt south of the present Gorge. Following this, in uppermost Miocene and lower Pliocene time, gentle folding of the crust formed basins which became shallow lakes both east (The Dalles area) and west (Portland and Tualatin areas) of the Cascades. At the same time Yakima Basalt flows in the Gorge area began to arch up. The basins filled with sediment as they subsided, until, in the Portland area, as much as 1000 feet of river and lake silt and clay *(Sandy River Mudstone)* was deposited. East of the mountains, debris from andesitic volcanoes together with erosional debris from the *Rhododendron Formation* was filling the basin to form *The Dalles Formation*.

The modern river emerges
(Pliocene — 5.0 to 1.8 my)

In earliest Pliocene, the course of the ancestral Columbia River was still a few miles south of the present Gorge, and the river was depositing, along its course and in the basins west of the Gorge, a floodwater deposit consisting of coarse gravels and sands *(Troutdale Formation)*. Most of the pebbles and cobbles, which filled in the ancient Columbia River Valley and the Portland basin to a depth of several hundred feet, were of locally derived basalts and andesites, but they also contained a widespread and unusual constituent composed of well rounded and polished pebbles and cobbles of *quartzite*. These metamorphic rocks must have made the thousand-mile trip from the Precambrian terranes in British Columbia. In a few places the quartzites make up 30 percent of the Troutdale conglomerate. The arrangement of these conglomerates invariably indicate a westward direction of the current in the 5 million-year-old ancestral river.

For perhaps a million years after the last outpouring of Columbia River Basalt there was relative quiet in the Gorge area, during which deep weathering, erosion and deposition in the broad basins along the Columbia River valley was the dominant geologic process. The final chapter in the location and development of the present Gorge was initiated by three processes, which so accelerated the pace of activity that a new chart on an expanded time scale is necessary to record the multitude of succeeding events (page 43).

The first of these processes, (volcanism) was a renewed outbreak in the Cascades of dozens of volcanos (Larch , Talapus,

Tanner, Green Point, Defiance, etc.) which built up great shields of gray basaltic lava and diverted the Columbia River northward to near its present course. During Pliocene and Quaternary time, the great composite volcanoes (Mt. Adams, Mt. Hood) also began their activity, which has continued down to the present, and literally hundreds of smaller basaltic volcanoes (Boring and Cascade lavas), began to dot the area (p. 42).

The second process (diastrophism) was the up-arching of the Coast Range and the Cascade region between the Willamette Valley and Hood River Valley which lifted the Troutdale gravels of the old Columbia Valley in the center of the arch to an elevation of 2700 feet, while the Portland basin continued its down folding. Between Hood River and The Dalles, similar

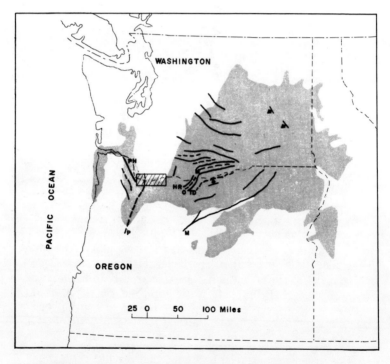

Folding of the Columbia River basalt. The Cascade arch in the Gorge is so broad and gentle that it is difficult to mark its crest. Both east and west in the Gorge, however, folds are better shown. Anticlines (arches) are solid lines, synclines (downwarps) are dashed. Some anticlines (west to east) include: PH: Portland Hills, HR: Hood River, O: Ortley (Columbia Hills), and M: Mitchell. Some synclines include: P: Portland, M: Mosier, TD: The Dalles.

forces folded the Yakima Basalts into a series of five anticlines and synclines, which are, from west to east; the Underwood (faulted) syncline, the Bingen anticline, the Mosier syncline, the Ortley anticline, and The Dalles syncline.

The third process (erosion) was the cutting by the Columbia River of a deep V-shaped canyon through these folds and the Cascade arch, keeping pace with the rise of the walls on either side. As the Gorge and its tributary valleys were cut down during the last five million years to present (and even below present) sea level, small volcanoes filled several of the tributary

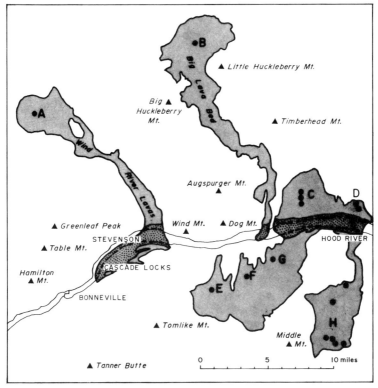

Quaternary intracanyon lava flows that reached the Gorge and may have dammed the river. Dotted pattern indicated where they have been eroded away. Volcanic sources are shown by dots, as follows: A. Trout Creek Hill, source of Carson or Wind River flow. B. Big Lava Flow crater, source of Little White Salmon River flow. C. Underwood Mountain vents. D. White Salmon vent. E. Mount Defiance. F. Viento Ridge vent. G. Mitchell Ridge vent. H. Cinder cones in the lower Hood River Valley.

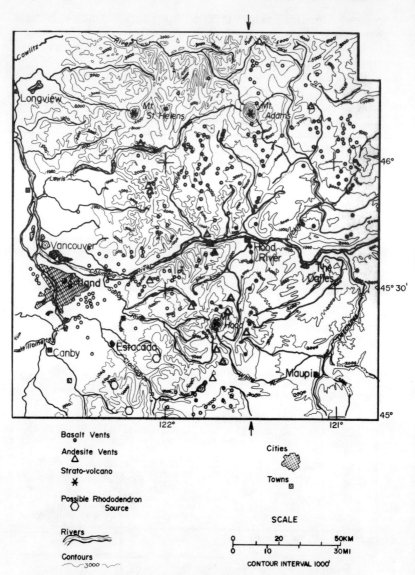

Basalt Vents
○

Andesite Vents
△

Strato-volcano
✳

Possible Rhododendron
○   Source

Rivers

Contours
~ 3000 ~

Cities

Towns

SCALE

0   20   50KM
0   10   30MI
CONTOUR INTERVAL 1000'

Volcanic centers in the Columbia River Gorge area. The more
than 250 centers mapped consist of 3 large stratovolcanoes,
3 possible centers of Rhododendron volcanism, 16 volcanoes
or stocks of andesitic composition, and more than 225 basaltic
vents. Note the north-south Mt. Adams alignment of nearly
40 vents parallel to the Hood River fault (see page 48) which
extends for 100 miles to the north and south edges of the
map (arrows).

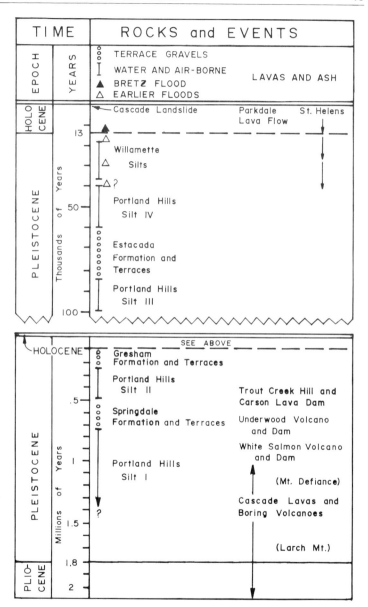

Quaternary time and rocks in the Columbia River Gorge. This is a continuation of the Tertiary stratigraphic column on page 35. Note that the lower part of the diagram is in millions and the upper part in thousands of years before the present. The *Portland Hills Silt* chronology is after Lentz (1977), the names of the terraces after Trimble (1963).

valleys with lava floods, several of which temporarily dammed
the river. At one point (Wind Mountain – Shellrock Mountain)
the river cut down through the roots of what may have been
a lower Pliocene volcano. This rise of the Cascade arch completed the climatic division of the Northwest into a western moist,
and an eastern dry section, governed by the now more or less
continuous mile-high elevation of the range.

Vegetation was becoming more like modern forms, with the
lush tropical forests of the lower Cenozoic of eastern Oregon
giving way to a cooler and semi-arid climate, causing extinction
of the metasequoia, magnolia, and other moist climate forms.
The horses had become larger and as the forests became grass-
lands, had changed from browsing to a grazing habit. Elephants
were beginning to be important in the moister western plains
which were now bordered by a sea which had retreated to much
the same position as today.

About 2 million years ago, the cooling of the climate accelerated, and the ice sheets began to form to the north. The Ice
Age or Pleistocene, which many believe is still with us, brought
on the last act of the drama.

Fire, ice and flood
(Pleistocene – 1.8 my to 12,000 years ago)

The Ice Age had more to do with shaping the present Columbia River Gorge than all the events during the previous tens
of millions of years. It brought into play a new geologic process,
that of *glaciation,* which was to indirectly affect the Gorge landscape in a number of ways.

For reasons still only imperfectly understood, the cooling climate, beginning about 2 million years ago, resulted in the formation of great ice sheets which eventually covered nearly a third
of the present land area of earth, and 55 percent of North America. The total amount of sea water piled up on land as ice in
the great ice caps was sufficient to lower sea level by at least
300 feet! This steepened the gradient of the lower Columbia
River, speeded up to rate of flow, and greatly increased the
power of the river to erode, so that the canyon was cut deep
below present sea level.

Actually, there were at least four major world-wide advances
and retreats of the ice sheets and consequent lowering of sea
level during the 2 my of the Ice Age. The last and greatest
reached a maximum about 40,000 years ago, when the western
(Cordilleran) sheet came down into eastern Washington as far
south as Spokane, and down the Puget Trough in western
Washington to beyond Tacoma and Olympia. During each of
these major advances of ice, the river returned to cutting the

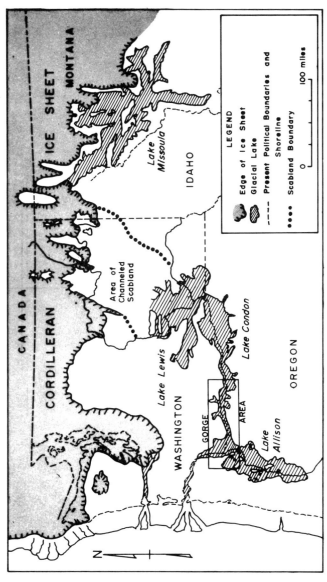

Glaciation, ice-age lakes and flooded areas (scabland when underlain by basalt) in the northwest. The maximum extent of the last ice sheet is shown by the hachured line. South of the ice, nearly 16,000 square miles was flooded or ponded in four temporary lakes: Missoula, Lewis, Condon and Allison. Note that the Pacific shoreline was many miles west of its present position, due to lowered sea level.

canyon below sea level; during the "interglacial" periods when the sea was near present sea level or even higher, the Gorge was filled with sand and gravel.

In addition to the ice sheets covering the northern part of the Columbia River drainage basin in Washington and Canada, hundreds of mountain glaciers clustered on the slopes of the higher volcanic peaks of the Cascade Range, occasionally spreading out to form small ice caps or extending down valleys to near sea level. Glaciers from Mt. Hood flowed 20 miles west down Sandy River canyon, and north down the upper tributaries of Hood River Valley. Ten glaciers still remain on upper slopes of Mount Hood.

At least 20 small glaciers less than 5 miles south of the Gorge carved small amphitheatres (cirques), many of them now occupied by tiny lakes, on the north and east sides of the ridges and peaks. None of these glaciers, which seldom came below an elevation of 3200 feet, were more than a mile in length; most of them were even smaller. The longest glacier near the Gorge was possibly the one which sculptured the northern side of Larch Mountain. Others cut into Palmer Peak, Mt. Talapus, and Tanner Butte. There were 5 glaciers around Mount Defiance and on Green Point Mountain.

North of the Gorge, Mt. St. Helens was built too late to be much affected by glaciers, but the older portions of Mount Adams were extensively sculptured by ice, and 9 glaciers still remain on that peak. Glacial valleys north of the Gorge, however, have been largely filled and masked by Quaternary volcanism.

All this excessive Pleistocene ice and snow pack meant an increase in the run-off so that during each spring and early summer rapid melting resulted most years in what would now be considered major floods. Since the ability of a stream to cut its channel increases many times faster than the volume of floodwater, most erosion is done by floods. Increased precipitation and the resulting annual floods during the Ice Age accomplished much of the cutting of the present Gorge and its tributary canyons. Most of the Gorge was already cut by half a million years ago, probably before catastrophic floods began. A 3500 foot-deep tributary canyon like Eagle Creek, eroded by spring floods during the Ice Age, would need to cut down at an average rate of only 4 inches per hundred years. Erosion by present-day Eagle Creek waters probably could not do this, a million heavy spring floods might easily do it.

Another important result of the activity of the ice sheets from the north was the production of incredible amounts of ground-up rock. Many cubic miles of material were gouged out of the

Canadian Rockies in eroding the hundreds of miles of U-shaped canyons of the northern Columbia River drainage basin.

For perhaps half a million summers the melting ice at the southern edge of the advancing and retreating ice front flowed brown and then milky with the slurry of rock particles. Then for another half million summers as well as during the dry and parched interglacial times, this silt and fine sand was picked up by the wind and spread over the surrounding hills south of the glaciated region. In eastern Washington it was deposited as the thick *Palouse Formation,* in the Portland area as the *Portland Hills Silt.* Both formations, although they contain some water-deposited layers, are largely loess, composed of silt-sized particles whose internal structure shows that it was deposited by the wind.

Terraces in the Portland area — Even the casual driver in east Portland will notice that the streets rise step-like as one goes east from the Willamette River, with a miie or more of "steps" between each "riser". The land surface near the Willamette River is at about 100 feet elevation (plus or minus 25 feet), the second step is at about 200 feet and the third at about 300 feet, and there is one even higher terrace south and east of Troutdale.

These steps are river terraces, formed by the cutting and filling of the Columbia River during and after the four or more glacial advances (and retreats of sea level). Early in the ice age, the Columbia and Sandy rivers in the Portland area meandered (looped back and forth) across the plain at an elevation several hundred feet higher than today.

The remnants of high terraces are the oldest, and now form relatively flat uplands which may cover wide areas. The surfaces of the terraces can be traced in the walls of the Sandy River valley for 20 miles from its mouth. As the land rose (or sea level lowered) the river successively cut the approximate 400, 300, and 200-foot surfaces, whose gravels were mapped by Trimble (1963) in the Portland area as the *Springwater, Gresham* and *Estacada Formations.* Elevations of these terrace rise upstream.

Faulting and earthquakes in the Gorge area — Fortunately, Oregon has no great 800-mile long active earthquake-producing fault like the San Andreas Rift of California. The movement of the two sides of this fault has generated most of the numerous earthquakes that from time to time harass Californians. There are numerous faults in the Gorge area, but most of them appear to be only a few miles long, and none of them have moved at the surface in historic times.

The longest fault that has been mapped along the lower Columbia River runs along the foot of the straight Portland Hills escarpment from Milwaukie northwest for at least 15 miles (Balsillie, 1971). It has a vertical displacement of at least 500 feet. No evidence of recent movement at the surface has been

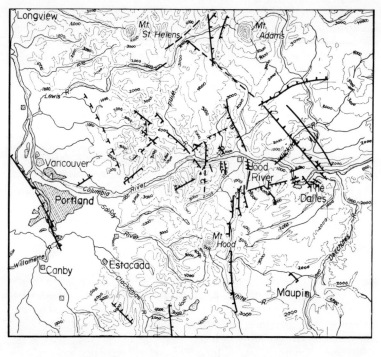

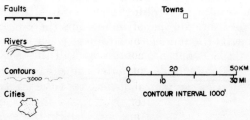

Faulting in the Columbia River Gorge area. Ticks are on the down-dropped side of the faults, arrows show direction of lateral movements. "Possible" faults are dashed or questioned (?). Of the faults to be seen, the Portland fault and the Hood River fault are the best known and show the greatest displacement. The Dog Mountain-Shellrock Mountain fault has been questioned by some geologists.

observed, although small earthquakes in 1949, 1962 and 1968 may have resulted from movements occurring on the fault several miles below the surface. It has been suggested that this fracture zone may also extend southeast up the Clackamas valley perhaps as far as central Oregon. If so it would be a major structure.

The north-south trending Hood River fault is another major structure, since it has been mapped intermittently for 60 miles in Oregon and Washington, and has a vertical displacement of nearly 2000 feet which forms the escarpment of the east wall of Hood River Valley.

Both of these fault escarpments commenced with earthquake movements that may have occurred as far back as the late Pliocene, but the relatively small amount of erosion of the escarpments suggests that most of the displacement has more probably occurred during the last half million years.

Indirect evidence for a possible large earthquake in the Gorge area lies in the great size (covering over 5 square miles) of the Cascade landslide, north of Bonneville. It has been suggested that it might have been triggered by an earthquake; the date of the slide has been established at about 1260 A.D. It will be discussed later.

The Catastrophic Floods — Towards the end of the Ice Age (50,000 to 12,000 years ago) a series of culminating catastrophies occurred in the Northwest, when nearly 16,000 square miles of the Columbia River drainage basin was repeatedly sculptured by some of the greatest floods known to man.* At least twice and possibly 40 times, advances of the ice sheet from Canada into northeastern Washington came far enough south to block the canyon of the Clark Fork River east of Lake Pend Oreille and form up to 1000-foot high ice dams. Behind the latest and probably the greatest of these dams there formed a 3000-square mile lake extending at 4000 feet elevation for 250 miles to the east into Montana, containing half the volume of Lake Michigan (500 cubic miles of water). (See page 45.)

When warming climate about 13,000 years ago reduced the height of the ice, and water overtopped the ice dam, it was swept away in a few hours and the last Bretz Flood* resulted.

---

*These were first called the "Spokane Floods" from their origin somewhere north of Spokane; then "Missoula Floods" from the lake which covered Missoula, Montana. Professor J.H. Bretz first described the features produced by the floods 50 years ago, the last and possibly the greatest of these floods should be named after him. When more than one flood is referred to, we will use "Spokane".

An estimated 380 cubic miles of water then poured out at a maximum rate of 9½ cubic miles per hour for at least 40 hours, over the Big Bend country of eastern Washington, sweeping southwesterly across the Columbia Plateau.

Ten times the combined flow of all the rivers of the world (60 times the flow of the Amazon River) carved out the soft silt (loess) and the basalt of the plateau beneath it into the multitude of dry coulees, falls, and barren channels which are characterized by the term "scablands".

The flood first ponded in the Pasco basin, the low point on the plateau, and formed Lake Lewis, it poured upstream and ponded in the Yakima, Walla Walla and Snake River valleys, and finally sought outlet down the Columbia River through the Wallula Gap into Oregon. It has been estimated that it came through the gap at a rate of 1.66 cubic miles of water an hour for two or three weeks. In comparison, the total water of the largest historical flood on the Columbia (1894) was about 2 cubic miles — the Bretz Flood was about 190 times this volume.

The flood crest at Wallula Gap was about 1200 feet; it spread out in Oregon to cover an area of 1300 square miles in the Umatilla Basin, called Lake Condon. The water poured down the Columbia, widening the valley and cleaning off all soil up to elevations of 1000 feet as far as The Dalles. Blocks and boulders of granite and schist were floated along, frozen in icebergs, to strand in tributary valleys. Hundreds of these "erratic" rocks have been found along the course of the flood. The lake in The Dalles Basin covered nearly 100 square miles, including the waters backed up in the valleys of Fifteenmile, Eightmile, Threemile, Mill and Chenowith Creeks. One large erratic was found at 970 feet elevation 10 miles from the mouth of Eightmile Creek. Deposits of poorly sorted gravels and lake silts occur in many of the tributary canyons along the Gorge up to elevations of 800 feet. In the Big Bend of the river at The Dalles, the flood removed substantial amounts of The Dalles Formation which once occupied much of the basin, and cut scabland channels and depressions into the underlying basalt, some to 225 feet below sea level! The lack of any soil below 1000 feet on the valley walls is still easily observed.

The flood overtopped the Mayer State Park viewpoint, and formed now dry channels at several points on its way to the Hood River Valley. At Hood River and downstream, there appears to be little evidence that the flood rose to over 900 feet, the highest erratic found in the Hood River valley is at 800 feet.

Between Mosier and Crown Point, the surface of the Bretz

flood dropped from 1000 to probably a little over 600 feet. The fact that many of the waterfalls in the walls of the Gorge top out at about 400 feet elevation, suggest that they are in part a result of the widening of the valley during this and preceding Spokane floods, which cut away the lower courses of the tributary streams and left high on the valley walls the hanging notches from which the falls depend.

The broad recessed alcoves in which the major falls lie could not have been formed by the floods or by water erosion, undercutting massive lava flows in zones of weakness in the rocks. They are undoubtedly the result of the influence of spray from the falls, seeping into the cracks of the finely jointed basalt and freezing and popping out the small brickbat sized blocks of basalt. Over the thousands of seasons during and since the upper Ice Age, the several hundred feet of retreat could easily be accomplished, since the shaded south wall of the Gorge could repeatedly freeze and thaw during winter months. Spring freshets could then remove the finer material collected at the base of the alcoves.

In the Willamette Valley, floodwaters poured out into the Portland area and spread south as far as Eugene, forming Lake Allison, which covered 3000 square miles. The waters rose, according to the evidence of erratics which have been found throughout the valley by Allison (1935), to almost 400 feet.

In summary, the approximate elevation of the Bretz flood as it passed through the Gorge was 1000 feet in the gap west of The Dalles, 900 feet just east of Hood River, 800 feet at Wind and Shellrock Mountains, 600 feet at Crown Point, and at 400 feet in the Willamette Valley. North of Mt. Scott only Mount Tabor, Rocky Butte and Kelly Butte stood above the waters.

The energy released by dropping 380 cubic miles of water from 4000 feet elevation to 300 feet below sea level, is equivalent to the explosions for 10 days of one fission bomb every four seconds, a hydrogen bomb every 36 minutes, or a Russian super bomb every 27 hours. If the flood came down during a 40 hour period, these would be multiplied by a factor of six.

If compared to the energy released by some major earthquakes, we get the following:

1½ times the energy generated by the largest known earthquake (M 8.6)

9½ times the Alaska earthquake (1964) M 8.4

191 times the San Francisco earthquake (1908) M 8.2

210,000 times the San Fernando earthquake (1972) M 6.2

19 million times the largest earthquake felt in Portland (1962) M 5

After the Ice
(13,000 years ago to Present)

The melting and retreat of the last of the northern ice sheets about 13,000 years ago caused sea level to rise at least 300 feet, and ushered in the final epoch of the Cenozoic, now called the Holocene or "completely recent."

This drowned the ice age coastal plain which was over 25 miles wide along the Oregon coast, but with a few volcanic exceptions other landscapes in northwestern Oregon can have changed very little during the 13 millenia since the last Bretz flood. The 300-foot deep inner canyon of the Columbia River was surely choked with debris left by the catastrophic floods. Erosion of this valley fill must have produced spectacular gravel cliffs along the river before they were eventually drowned by the later melting of the ice sheets and slow inland advance of the tidal waters, and the inner canyon refilled by normal annual floods.

Volcanic activity — In Holocene time, only a few basaltic cinder cones erupted short lava flows (as in upper Hood River valley, and far south in the McKenzie pass area) and the high peaks of the Cascades continued spasmodic outbursts of ash and cinders. Mount St. Helens is an exception, since, although its history extends back more than 37,000 years, virtually the entire visible volcano has formed since about 500 B.C., and most of the upper part has been built within the last few hundred years. Since about 2500 B.C., it is probable that the volcano has never been dormant more than about five centuries at a time. Mount Hood has also erupted during the last few thousand years.

Landslides — The other catastrophic activities of special importance in the Gorge were the landslides, especially along the unstable north side of the river between Cape Horn and Dog Mountain. Here the bedrock consists of the old ash and mudflow deposits of the Eagle Creek and Ohanapecosh Formations rather than of the more resistant Yakima Basalt. The valley walls had been undercut and their slopes steepened by the Spokane floods so that they were already relatively unstable. Slides could be triggered (as they still are today) by periods of excessive rainfall or by earthquakes. (See page 54.)

The largest slide area covers nearly 14 square miles north of Bonneville, and is composed of several lobes, totalling over half a cubic mile of material, which came down at different times. The lobe of the latest ("Cascade") slide covers about 5½ square miles. It diverted the river a mile to the south, and continued as a dam long enough, in all probability, to give rise

Recent (about 7000 years ago) flow of basalt from small cinder cone in upper Hood River Valley west of Parkdale. Looking north, the source in the foreground (Sam Sargent photo)

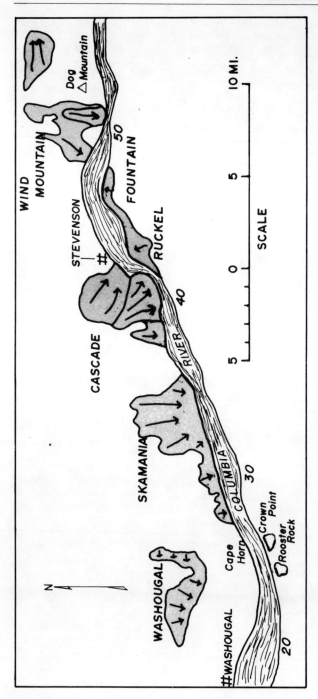

Landslides cover an area of about 50 square miles within and near the Columbia River Gorge. The Cascade slide dammed the river about 1260 A.D., the remnants of the dam formed the Cascades of the Columbia before the building of Bonneville dam. Part of the Wind Mountain slide is moving today up to 45 feet per year.

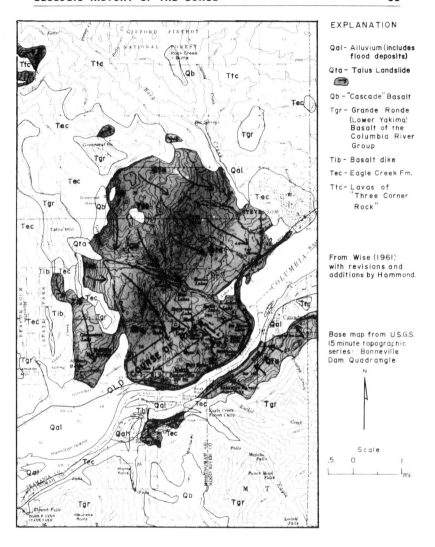

EXPLANATION

Qal- Alluvium (includes
flood deposits)

Qta – Talus Landslide

Qb – "Cascade" Basalt

Tgr – Grande Ronde
(Lower Yakima)
Basalt of the
Columbia River
Group

Tib – Basalt dike

Tec - Eagle Creek Fm.

Ttc- Lavas of
"Three Corner
Rock"

From Wise (1961)
with revisions and
additions by Hammond.

Base map from U.S.G.S.
15 minute topographic
series: Bonneville
Dam Quadrangle.

N

Scale
.5   0   1
| | | |mi.

The Cascade landslide at Bonneville, with surrounding geology. There have been at least four separate slide lobes of
varying size, totalling about 14 square miles of disturbed
ground. Heavy Grande Ronde (Tgr) Basalt flows cap
Greenleaf Peak and Table Mountain, resting upon 1000 feet
of weak, clay-bearing Eagle Creek (Tec) sediments. Note the
pre-1260 A.D. course of the river, now covered by the lobe
that produced the Cascades of the Columbia (and the Bridge
of the Gods?).

to the Indian legend of the "Bridge of the Gods." When it was
overtopped and largely washed away by water from the lake
that formed behind it, it left the Cascades of the Columbia,
which later proved to be such a trial to early travelers in the
Gorge and gave the name to the mountain range. Dating by
C^{14} radioactive analysis made on tree stumps (Lawrence, 1958)
indicates that the slide occurred about 1260 A.D., possibly triggered by a large earthquake. Remnants of the forest drowned
by the temporary 300-foot deep lake could be seen at low water
for tens of miles upstream, before both the Cascades and the
stumps were submerged by the waters behind Bonneville dam.

Lewis and Clark, the first explorers to pass through the Gorge,
noted the drowned trees and correctly deduced their origin. On
the return trip, April 14, 1806, Meriwether Lewis reports:

"Throughout the whole course of the river from the
rapids as high as the Chillickittiquas, we find the trunks
of many large pine trees standing erect as they grew at
present in 30 feet of water; they are much doated and none
of them vegetating; at the lowest tide of the river many
of these trees are in ten feet of water. Certain it is that
those large pine trees never grew in that position, nor can
I account for this phenomenon except it be that the passage
of the river through the narrow pass at the rapids has been
obstructed by the rocks which have fallen from the hills
into that channel ..."

Another still active slide on the north side of the river lies
just east of Wind Mountain, where about 3 square miles is moving as much as 47 feet per year. Of the slides on the south
side of the river, the Ruckel slide, near Cascade Locks, started
moving when the railroad was first being built in 1877, and
kept moving intermittently until 1918 when drainage tunnels
were completed. Four miles east of Cascade Locks, the Fountain
slide has continually disrupted and uplifted the highway for
the last 25 years, and removal by the highway department of
more than 3 million cubic yards of overburden has failed to
stop the movement.

Catastrophic events in the Columbia River Gorge.
Catastrophe: "a sudden and violent change in the surface
of the earth" (Webster). The table summarizes at least 150
events resulting from lava flows, mud flows, ash falls, landslides and floods during the last 40 million years.

PERIOD	CATASTROPHIC EVENTS	Chronology (years ago)	Height of dams or floods (feet)	Number of episodes
QUATERNARY	Cascade (Bonneville) landslides	750 others older	400	3 plus
	Bretz (Spokane, Missoula) floods	13,000 30,000 others older	600 to 1000	2 to 7?
	Wind River lava dams, lakes	Older than	400 1000	2
	Little White Salmon River lava dams, lake	25,000 and less than	700	1
	Underwood Mountain-Mt. Defiance lava dams, lakes	700,000	1000	2?
	(Modern gorge first appears)			
TERTIARY	Boring – Cascade volcanoes	1 to 4 my		100 plus
	Troutdale torrential floods	3 to 5 my		5 plus
	Rhododendron volcanism	6 to 7 my		2 ?
	Columbia River basalt floods	10 to 17 my		About 18 flows
	Eagle Creek mud flows	20 to 22 my		5 plus
	Ohanapecosh ash, mud and lava flows	30 to 40 my		numerous

CHAPTER 4:
MAN IN THE GORGE

"Historians explain the past and economists
predict the future. Thus only the present is
confusing"

(Anonymous)

During the last glacial lowering of sea-level, man certainly
crossed over into North America on the Alaska land-bridge from
Asia probably as long as 35,000 years ago. (Recent evidence is
beginning to suggest that he may even have entered the Americas as much as 100,000 years ago!) Within a few thousand years
he must have spread widely over the continent, but left little
evidence of his occupation in the northwest until about 10,000
years ago. Evidence of these Folsom and Marmes men (from
a site on the lower Snake River in Washington) have been found
in a large number of digs in the western United States.

Excavations at Five Mile Rapids a few miles east of The
Dalles (now covered by water above the dam) showed that man
continuously occupied this ideal fishing site just east of the
Gorge for the last 10,000 years. He may indeed have lived there
in still earlier times, and have reoccupied the site after each
catastrophic Spokane flood!

Man has been considered the most dangerous animal ever
to inhabit the earth. Can it be only a coincidence that 9 of
the 17 species of large North American ice age mammals became
extinct during the geologically short period from 10 to 5 thousand years ago? Only the caribou, elk, moose, bison, mountain
sheep goat, antelope and deer, survived into modern times.

A capsule history of man in the Gorge

31,000 B.C. circa   Early Spokane catastrophic floods. Man ar-
                                 rived in North America at least this far
                                 back.

18,000 B.C. circa   Man widespread in both the Americas.

13,000 B.C. circa   Last Bretz catastrophic flood, water from 400 to 1000 feet deep in the Gorge, 190 times larger than greatest historic flood.

8000 B.C. circa   Early (Marmes and Wakemap) man occupied the area, with salmon probably their chief subsistence for the succeeding 10,000 years. Extinction of many large North American mammals began about this time, and was almost complete by 3000 B.C.

5000 B.C. circa   Parkdale lava flow in upper Hood River valley.

1260 A.D. circa   Cascade landslide at Bonneville produced the Cascades of the Columbia, the temporary dam probably resulting in the Indian legend of the "Bridge of the Gods."

1726   Most recent eruption of Mount Hood.

1780   Smallpox epidemic decimated indians.

1792   Captain Gray first crossed the bar of the Columbia, and named it after his ship. Lt. William R. Broughton took a boat up river as far as the mouth of the Sandy River, and named Mount Hood, after Vice Admiral Samuel Lord Hood of The British Navy.

1805-1806   Meriwether Lewis and George Clark were the first white men to traverse the Gorge. Made the first maps; named Beacon Rock and many other geographic features.

1812   William Price Hunt (Astor party), David Thompson, Alexander Ross, and Gabriel Franchere traversed the Gorge.

1823-1824   David Douglas climbed Hamilton Mountain north of Beacon Rock, and the cliffs across the river.

1825   Fort Vancouver established.

1830-1835	Pestilence killed more than half the 80,000 indians along the Columbia.
1832	Nathaniel Wyeth brought an early group of settlers down the river.
1833 and 1840	River frozen over.
1841	70 pioneer immigrants, came down the river; in 1842 over 100 more.
1842	River frozen over.
1842-1849	Mount St. Helens active on and off for seven years.
1843	Years of the "Great Migration," over 800 immigrants came down the river. Champoeg government established. Rev. Gustavus Hines attributed the Cascades to a landslide. During a great flood, water rose 11 feet higher at The Dalles than in the 1894 flood.
1844	First portage wagon road around the Cascades replaced the portage trail on the north side.
1846	Palmer Pack Trail around the Cascades for cattle and horses built on south side. The Barlow Road was built south of Mount Hood. The Canadian boundary established by the Treaty of Ghent.
1847-1848	Whitman massacre and reprisals.
1848	Oregon Territory established.
1848	The pack trail on the south side was improved for wagons for use during the summer. The greatest obstacle was Tooth Rock (now tunneled near Bonneville).
1850	First steamboat "The Columbian" to travel the river above the Cascades.

1851	Wooden portage railroad built at Cascades on north side; first mail deliveries from Salt Lake City; post offices established at the Cascades, The Dalles, and Camas.
1853	Washington Territory established.
1855-1856	Yakima Indian War and "Cascades Massacre."
1858	Wooden portage railroad replaces wagon road on south side.
1861-1870	Eastern Oregon gold rush. Led to rapid expansion of navigation on the river for more supplies to miners and gold back to Portland.
1862-1862	First steam locomotive, the "Oregon Pony", replaced mules on the south side portage. First steel-railed railroad on north side portage.
1862-1873	Thomas Condon, pioneer Oregon geologist, lived in The Dalles, and did the first geological investigations in the Gorge.
1872	The legislature appropriated $50,000 for a road from Troutdale to The Dalles. It was not completed for 43 years!
1878	Construction of Cascade Locks and canal started. Took 20 years to complete!
1879	Fish wheel era started; wheels used to harvest the enormous runs of salmon, era was to last for 55 years.
1879-1883	Post offices established at Carson, Washougal, Skamania, and Cape Horn. The "Harvest Queen" 846 tons, built at Celilo. It was the largest sternwheeler on the upper river.
1880	First train from Portland to Bonneville.

1881	Rebuilding of the portage railroad on the south side, after floods took out the bridge around the base of Tooth Rock.
1883	Completion of the Oregon Railway and Navigation Company Railroad on the south side.
1884	Starvation Creek named, when train with 148 passengers was stalled by snow slides for 4 days, and took 3 weeks to reach Portland. River frozen over from mouth to the Cascades.
1888	River frozen over.
1890	The sternwheeler "Harvest Queen" shot the Cascade rapids to the delight of hundreds of spectators. Frederick Balche's novel "Bridge of the Gods" published.
1890-1891	Big freeze stopped all navigation on the river.
1894	Largest flood on record; 125 million cubic feet per second (normal averages 262,000) or five times normal flow. Stevenson post office established.
1896	Completion of Cascade Locks and canal, permitting through steamboat traffic, which previously could only rarely run the Cascades during high water. Columbia River frozen over at The Dalles.
1900-1910	Period of large scale logging. Virgin Douglas fir in the Gorge largely logged off.
1902	First Yacolt fire burned half a million acres north of the river. This is equivalent to nearly 800 square miles, or an area 28 miles square. Later great fires in 1910 and 1929 totalled 25 million acres burned, about 4000 square miles, or an area 200 miles square.

1905-1920	Period of large scale fishing by means of salmon wheels, with consequent elimination of the great salmon runs.
1908	First automobile and first train to arrive from Vancouver in Stevenson, and completion of S.P. and S.R.R. on north side of river.
1915	Completion of the Columbia River Scenic Highway, with Samuel C. Lancaster as engineer.
1916	First detailed report on the geology of the Columbia River Gorge by Ira Williams. Sternwheeler "Tahoma" frozen in ice near Cape Horn for 5 weeks!
1919	River frozen over.
1920	Completion of Evergreen Highway, Washington 14, on north side.
1924	River frozen over
1926	Completion of the "Bridge of the Gods" highway bridge at Cascade Locks. In 1940 it was raised 40 feet.
1930	River frozen over.
1933	Construction of Bonneville Dam started.
1937	Lowest river flow on record; 35,000 cubic feet per second.
1938	Completion of Bonneville Dam, drowning of the Cascades of the Columbia.
1946	Landslide of 300,000 cubic yards half a mile east of Multnomah Falls.
1948	Vanport flood, last major flood in lower Columbia River.

1956	Completion of The Dalles Dam; drowning the Chutes, Narrows, and the Celilo canal.
1964	Severe winter floods.
1970	Mini-glacier formed below Multnomah Falls during January cold spell.
1975	Completion of the last stretch of the I-80-N Freeway.
1977	Driest year in recorded history. Without the dams, the flow of the Columbia would have been much lower than the previous 1937 record.

PART II
HIGHWAY GUIDES

"He who with pocket-hammer smites the edge
Of luckless rock or prominent stone, disguised
In weather-stains or crusted o'er by Nature,
The substance classes by some barbarous name
And thinks himself enriched,
Wealthier, and doubtless wiser than before."

William Wordsworth, *The Excursion,* (1814)

CHAPTER 1:
HOW TO GET MOST
OUT OF THE ROAD LOGS

The following trips point out geologic features, works of man, occasional historical items and something of the vegetation. The trips are NOT designed for the lone driver, who dares not (or at least should not!) crane his neck to observe scenery in all directions. Most of the features noted can be seen by passengers from the car, but it will often be better to park at the suggested points of interest (STOP), get out and walk a few feet. While driving, the front seat passenger should be charged with following the trip log and keeping track of mileages. Mileages are continuous from the beginning to the end of each trip. Remember that the highway mileposts on the Scenic Highway do not correspond to the mileposts which on I 80 record miles from the Willamette River in Portland.

At the end of the discussion of each feature, the distance to the next point is given, so that the reader may anticipate the approaching scenery or geologic feature.

In order to know *where* to look for points of interest, the "o'clock" system is used, with the front of the car as 12:00, the rear as 6:00, omitting the word "o'clock". The diagram below illustrates the system:

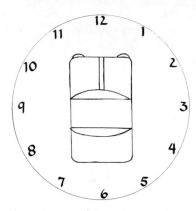

If you have read Part I, you will have a considerable background in "what to look for" in the Portland area and on the highways through the Gorge. But reading is only the first step (a necessary one, since "one sees only what one is looking for") and seeing and recognizing the actual rocks and landforms that have been discussed is where the real fun comes in.

A fairly detailed description of the actual physical appearance and composition of the various formations and rock assemblages that are mentioned in the road logs is given in the following stratigraphic column. Remember, you are reading down from youngest to oldest!

STRATIGRAPHIC COLUMN
SURFICIAL DEPOSITS

Quaternary Alluvium (Holocene)

Loose deposits of silt, sand and gravel bordering the Columbia River and its tributaries, usually less than 50 feet above water level. Includes some sand dunes, as the ridge east of Rooster Rock State Park.

Quaternary Landslide Debris (mostly Holocene)

Surficial slide deposits associated with large landslides, and composed of boulders and finer debris mostly derived from the Eagle Creek Formation and overlying lava flows. Best developed north of the river.

Quaternary Flood Deposits and Lake Beds

Unconsolidated gravel, sand, silt and clay deposited during the latest Pleistocene advances of the ice in northern Washington, by the torrential waters of the Missoula (Spokane) floods, especially the last Bretz flood. Contains widespread angular ice-rafted erratic boulders up to 8 feet in diameter. Forms high bars along the river, particularly behind promontories and within reentrants and up tributaries, and mantles much of the Portland and Vancouver area below 400 feet in elevation.

Quaternary Terrace Deposits (mostly Pleistocene)

Flat-lying elevated deposits of gravel, sand and silt of fluvial (river) and glacio-fluvial origin, best developed along the Sandy River and in east Portland. Divided by Trimble (1963) on the basis of elevation and degree of weathering into the *Springwater* (highest and oldest), *Gresham* (intermediate), and *Estacada* (lowest and youngest) *Formations*. Of equivalent age, mantling much of the topography above 400 feet, is the *Portland Hills Silt,* a yellowish-brown loess (wind-blown silt) which is chiefly quartzose, with minor sand and clay; greatest thickness is 145 feet, averages less than 25 feet. It is thickest over the Portland Hills and on the Springwater Terrace, and has been divided into three units.

STRATIGRAPHIC UNITS

Pliocene and Quaternary Volcanic Rock

Up to several thousand feet of lava flows and minor amounts of cinders and breccias of dominantly basaltic composition. Usually light gray in color, frequently porous (diktytaxitic). Includes the *Cascade Lavas* (sometimes andesitic) which form the thin flows in the upper cliffs on the south wall of the Gorge beneath the upland surface, and the shield volcanos which rise above that surface; the *Boring Lavas* from numerous cinder cones in the Portland area; and the young *Intracanyon Lavas* which lie in valleys tributary to the Gorge. Flows are generally less than 50 feet thick, except where ponded in narrow canyons.

Pliocene Sedimentary Rock

Up to 1400 feet of fluvial deposits of mudstone, sandstone, siltstone, conglomerate and volcaniclastic materials, occupying structural depressions and erosional valleys in Yakima Basalt. Overlain by Cascade and Boring Lavas west of Hood River. Includes the *Troutdale Formation,* best exposed along the Sandy River, in the Portland Basin and in the south wall of the Gorge; *The Dalles Formation* in and around The Dalles and Mosier basins; the *Rhododendron Formation* in the south wall of the Gorge between Tanner and Herman Creeks; and the *Sandy River Mudstone,* which underlies the Troutdale conglomerate in the Portland basin, but is not exposed in the Gorge. The Troutdale conglomerate contains high percentages of basalt and andesite pebbles, but also sometimes high concentrations of exotic quartzite pebbles and occasional pebbles of granite, schist and other non-volcanic rocks that could only have been derived from the Precambrian and Paleozoic metamorphic terrain of British Columbia. The Dalles and Rhododendron rocks are dominantly andesitic to dacitic volcaniclastic debris, which also makes up much of the matrix between the pebbles, and may form interbeds in the Troutdale. South of the Gorge, Rhododendron may underlly Troutdale as well as Cascade Lavas.

Yakima Basalt of the Columbia River Group (Middle Miocene) Up to 2000 feet of dense, flow-on flow, usually black, glassy basalt, in flows less than 100 feet thick, forming the major cliffs in the Gorge. Includes interbeds of soil as at Oneonta Gorge and pillow lavas as at Multnomah Falls and east of Crown Point and The Dalles. Extends many miles south of the Gorge beneath Cascade Lavas and Rhododendron Formation and west of the Gorge beneath Troutdale. On the north side of the Gorge west of Hood River it occurs only in isolated patches less than 10 miles from the river. Erupted from 12 to 16 million years ago from dike swarms far to the east. Has been divided by Swanson (1976) into three formations: a lower *Grandé Ronde Basalt,* to which nearly all the flows west of Mosier belong; a middle *Wanapum Basalt* east of Mosier and beneath Crown Point; and an upper *Saddle Mountain Basalt* in the Mosier basin.

Eagle Creek Formation (Lower Miocene) Up to 1000 feet of poorly sorted volcanic sediments of torrential and mudflow origin, mostly andesitic conglomerates, breccias and tuffs containing some carbonaceous swamp sediments. Best exposed between McCord and Eagle Creeks, and in the high cliffs of Hamilton and Table Mountains and Greenleaf Peak. North of Stevenson, patches of Eagle Creek rest upon a red-weathered paleosoil developed upon the underlying lavas.

*Lavas of Three-Corner Rock (Lower Miocene) Up to 3000 feet of interbedded andesitic lava flows, breccias and tuffs, best exposed north and east of Stevenson between Rock Creek and Wind River. Also occurs high on the mountain north of Beacon Rock. Formerly considered to be part of the Ohanapecosh Formation, now thought to be part of the Fife's Peak Group of central Washington.

Stevens Ridge Formation (Mostly Upper Oligocene)
From 50 to 5000 feet of chiefly varicolored tuffs and a few sandstones and conglomerates. Occurs several miles north of Dog Mountain and northwest of Beacon Rock. Formerly considered to be part of the Ohanapecosh Formation.

Ohanapecosh Formation (Mostly Lower Oligocene)
These oldest rocks exposed in the Gorge appear above river level only on the north side, around and north of Camas and Washougal (where it has been called the Skamania Volcanics), and east of Wind River, where they are more than a mile thick. Farther northwest they may total more than two miles in thickness. Like the two overlying formations, the Ohanapecosh lavas, volcaniclastic breccias and tuffs are more andesitic than basaltic, and characteristically exhibit greenish and reddish colors, a result of the pervasive and widespread development of low-grade metamorphic zeolitic and argillic minerals.

IGNEOUS INTRUSIONS
Tertiary Intrusions (Mostly Pliocene)
Stocks of fine-grained quartz diorite at and north of Wind and Shellrock Mountains and east of Cascade Locks, and the basalt plugs or dike at and north of Beacon Rock. May have been feeders to Pliocene lava flows now worn away in the cutting of the Gorge.

---

*These two formations, recently described and mapped by Hammond (1979), are included in the text with the *Ohanapecosh* Formation.

PLANNING THE TRIP

The nearly 200-mile round trip can be shortened in a number of ways. One can cross the river and return to Portland or Vancouver at the Cascade Locks Bridge of the Gods, a 100-mile loop; or at Hood River, a 140-mile loop. One can skip the Scenic Highway and save 5 miles by staying on the Freeway.

On the other hand, there are several additional side trips well worthy of consideration:

26 mile round trip to the summit of Larch Mountain

9 mile scenic side trip from Mosier to Rowena

6 mile scenic side trip west of Lyle and the Klickitat River

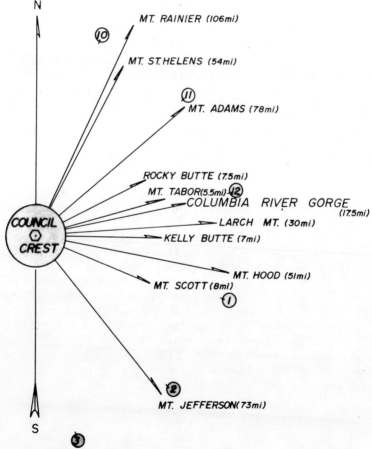

Orientation diagram for features visible on a clear day from Council Crest. Compare with map which shows the location of the nearby volcanos. Distances are shown in parenthesis. The Columbia River Gorge is taken as 12:00.

The best place to orient oneself before beginning the trip through the Gorge is to visit on a clear day the summit of the Portland Hills, at the view circle in Council Crest Park. One can see on the distant skyline five High Cascade volcanoes, from Mount Rainier, 106 miles to the north to Mount Jefferson, 73 miles south. Even when visibility is less clear, numerous older Boring volcanoes can be seen rising above the terraced east Portland plain. Rocky Butte, Mount Tabor, Kelly Butte and Mount Scott are only the most visible four of over 40 volcanic vents in and around Portland. At least 6 volcanoes lie a mile or so west of the crest of the Portland Hills, in a northwest-trending line over 10 miles long. Mount Sylvania, upon which Portland Community College rests, is the largest of these.

Council Crest is located at 1065 feet elevation near the crest of the northwest-trending Portland Hills anticline, underlain by about 1000 feet of Columbia River Basalt. The Portland Hills fault lies near the base of the east escarpment of Portland Hills. The broad, 13-mile wide valley between the Willamette and Sandy Rivers is in a northwest-trending syncline, where the top of the basalt drops to 1500 feet below sea level. This basin is filled with Sandy River Mudstone beneath Troutdale gravel, and covered with a skim of river terrace gravels and lake and flood deposits. The Yakima Basalt of the Portland Hills anticline is partly covered with a mantle of Portland Hills Silt, a fine-grained silt or loess that was washed in during the Ice Age and blown up over the hills during arid periods. When saturated during extended periods of heavy rain, it is the cause of most of the landslide and mudflow damage which plagues residents on the steep slopes of the Hills.

The surface of the east Portland plains, as well as the Vancouver plains north across the Columbia River, were swept by the waters of the Spokane floods, washing away most of the silt below 400 feet elevation, and scouring out channels and closed depressions. These are especially evident near Rocky Butte, as will be pointed out on the trip.

Now you are ready to take off on the trip. Pack a lunch to eat in one of the 30 parks en route. Take it easy and drive carefully!

Boring volcanoes southeast of Portland, with Mount Hood on the skyline. At least 10 vents are visible in this picture. (Ore. Dept. of Transp. photo).

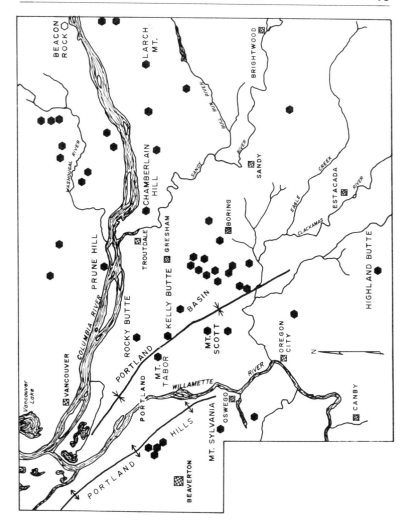

Location of the nearly 50 Boring Volcanoes in the Portland area. Larch Mountain, Highland Butte and Mount Sylvania near the east, south and west edges of the map, are all large low domes known as "shield volcanoes." The rest are cinder cones seldom rising more than a thousand feet above their base. Their characteristic internal structure and composition can be best seen in a quarry face in Mount Tabor Park. All these volcanoes are probably less than 5 my old.

LOCATION OF PARKS
(En route, Scenic Highway between Portland and The Dalles)

Road log miles at exit	Mileage finder
0.0	Council Crest City Park
3.1	(OMSI-Zoo-Forestry Center-0.3m.)
10.6	(Mount Tabor City Park-0.8m.)
20.5	(Blue Lake County Park -2.4m.)
22.5	Exit 18, Leave Freeway
22.9	Lewis & Clark State Park
26.0	Dabney State Park
31.4	Womens Forum State Park
31.8	(Larch Mountain Forest Park -13m)
32.6	Crown Point State Park
34.9	Talbot S.P. (Latourelle Falls)
36.1	Shepperds Dell State Park
40.3	Wahkeena Falls State Park
40.8	Multnomah Falls Forest Park
43.0	Oneonta Falls and Gorge
43.3	Horsetail Falls
43.8	Ainsworth State Park (Day-Use)
44.4	*Ainsworth Campground
45.0	Reenter Freeway
46.8	John B. Yeon State Park
49.6	(Bonneville Dam -1.8m.)
50.9	*Eagle Creek Forest Park
51.1	Sheridan Wayside
52.8	(*Cascade Locks County Park-1.4m.)
56.8	Lang State Park
64.1	Lindsey Creek State Park
65.6	Starvation Creek State Park
66.4	*Viento State Park
68.5	Wygant State Park
69.6	Lausman State Park
72.9	(*Tucker County Park -5m.)
78.8	(Mayer State Park -7m.)
81.8	Memaloose State Park (Rest Area)
85.7	(*Memaloose State Park -4m.)
85.7	(Mayer State Park - 2m.)
95.9	(The Dalles Dam -3m.)

Alphabetical finder

43.8	Ainsworth (Day Use)
	*Ainsworth (Camp-
44.4	ground)
20.3	(Blue Lake)
49.6	(Bonneville Dam)
52.8	(*Cascade Locks)
0.0	Council Crest
32.6	Crown Point
26.0	Dabney
50.9	*Eagle Creek
43.3	Horsetail
46.8	John B. Yeon
56.8	Lang
31.8	(Larch Mountain)
69.6	Lausman
22.9	Lewis & Clark
34.9	Latourelle (Talbot)
64.1	Lindsey Creek
85.5	(Mayer 78.8 or)
85.7	(*Memaloose)
81.8	Memaloose Rest Area
10.6	(Mount Tabor)
40.8	Multnomah
43.0	Oneonta
3.1	(OMSI-Zoo)
10.6	(Mount Tabor)
51.1	Sheridan
36.1	Shepperds Dell
65.6	Starvation Creek
34.9	Talbot
95.9	(The Dalles Dam)
72.9	(*Tucker)
66.4	*Viento
40.3	Wahkeena
31.4	Womens Forum
68.5	Wygant

Location of Parks, en route between Portland and The Dalles. There are over 30 parks, rest stops, viewpoints and other places of interest, Asterisks (*) refer to parks with camping facilities; Parentheses ( ) refer to parks off the main route, with distance from the exit.

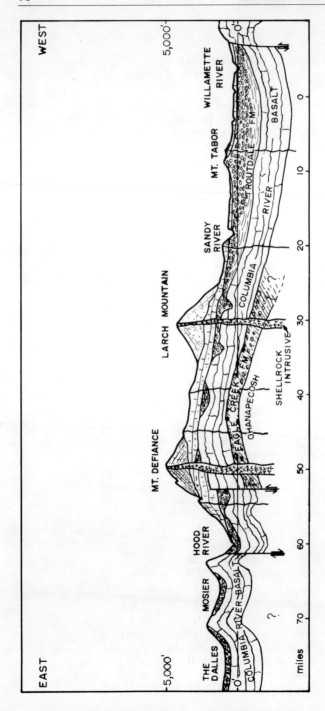

Diagrammatic "cross-section" from Portland to The Dalles, showing the relative positions and attitudes of the geologic formations which may be seen on the south side of the Gorge. Note that the vertical scale is exaggerated about 10 times. See page 113 for a similar sketch of the north side of the Gorge.

CHAPTER 2
GEOLOGIC ROAD LOG:

Portland to The Dalles Junction via Highway I-80 and the Scenic Highway 30

0.0   STOP. Council Crest Circle. See previous discussion. (0.3)

0.3   Stop sign, turn left. Note bumpy pavement within next quarter mile, produced by landsliding in Portland Hills Silt. (0.3)

0.6   Turn left beneath overpass. (0.1)

.7   Continue straight ahead. Jct. with Talbot Rd. (0.2)

.9   Junction with Patton Road. Keep straight ahead on Humphrey Boulevard scenic drive. (0.2)

1.1   Note Washington Park across valley at 3:00, with museum, zoo and forestry center, all located upon a great ancient landslide scar. (0.3)

1.4   Another view across valley. (0.9)

2.3   Junction at Sylvan with Skyline Boulevard and Sunset Highway, No. 26. Turn towards Portland. (0.7)

3.0   Approaching Washington Park landslide. Heavy riprap on the left just beyond the overpass, was emplaced in order to prevent further sliding. (0.1)

3.1   Zoo-Omsi exit. For the next five miles, keep to the right hand lane, over the Marquam Bridge, and onto the exit to I-80 N, towards The Dalles. (2.9)

6.0   Crossing Marquam Bridge, keep in right lane. (1.0)

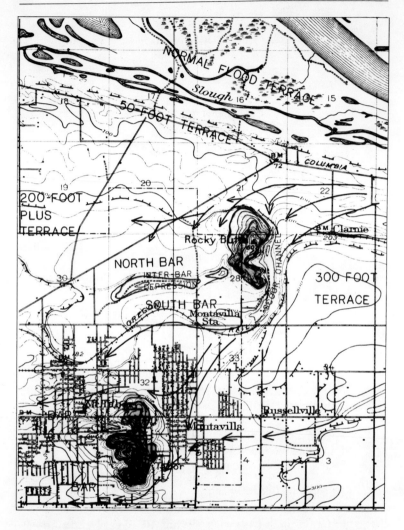

Topographic map of 1896 showing deep closed depressions (hachured contour lines) around Rocky Butte. These channels were gouged out about 13,000 years ago by swift currents (shown by arrows), of the Bretz flood diverted south around the butte. Rocky Butte, like a pebble on the beach washed by a retreating wave, developed channels on the upstream side as well as between two "tail-bars" built up west of the butte. Floodwaters reached the 400-foot contours, covering all the map except the shaded area. To some extent they also sculptured the 200-foot and 300-foot terraces whose edges are shown by dashed lines with tick-marks.

7.0   Turn right on I-80 towards The Dalles. We will be on I-80 for next 15 miles, leaving after we cross the Sandy River, east of Troutdale. (1.4)

8.4   Milepost 1. (2.2)

10.6   57th St. exit. Mt. Tabor Park and volcano is 0.8 miles south on 60th St. (0.3)

10.9   Note Mt. Tabor volcano on right at 3:00. The freeway has followed Sullivans Gulch since leaving the Willamette River. (1.3)

12.2   82nd Street exit. Approaching the flood scour channel (in part closed depression) which sweeps around the east and south side of Rocky Butte, oversteepening the east wall of this small volcano. (0.4)

12.6   Crossing scour channel in next mile. (0.2)

12.8   Halsey Street exit. Rocky Butte, on the left although composed largely of Boring-type vesicular gray olivine basalt, as exposed in the cliffs across the channel, also has red cinders in road cuts at the south summit. An abandoned quarry on the northwest side exposes a feeder column of lava cutting up through Troutdale conglomerate, the bedding of which has been slightly arched by the intrusion. The east side was scoured away by the Spokane floods, which also eroded much of the channel-way of Sullivan's Gulch. (0.9)

13.7   102nd Street exit. 275-foot terrace forms crest of ridge to right of highway. (1.2)

14.9   122nd Street exit. You are still travelling just below edge of 275-foot terrace on right. (0.9)

15.8   Lower terraces of the valley of the Columbia River on left; entrance to Gorge is visible on a clear day at 11:00, Larch Mountain shield volcano may be seen on the skyline at 12:00. (4.7)

20.5   Wood Village-Gresham exit to Mount Hood highway. (0.2)

20.7   Descending to 75-foot terrace, underlain by Pleistocene alluvium. (0.6)

21.3   Descending to lowest terrace, on Recent alluvium. Reynolds Aluminum plant at 9:00, 275-foot terrace (here actually above 300 feet) on skyline at 3:00. On skyline at 1:00 is Chamberlain Hill volcano (Boring age). The bluff beneath is of Troutdale gravels, capped by an upper 100 feet of lava. (0.5)

21.8   Troutdale exit 17. Continue ahead. Chamberlain Hill at 1:00 o'clock. Note "arches" caused by radial jointing in Boring lava in upper part of Broughton Bluff across the river. These are thought to be filled lava tubes. The contact between the lava and the underlying Troutdale is covered here by talus and landslide. (0.4)

22.3   Sandy River Bridge. Slow down, prepare to turn on Scenic Highway. (0.2)

22.5   Take exit 18, turn right off Freeway beyond bridge to Lewis and Clark State Park. Turn left at stop. (0.2)

22.7   At 3:00 to 6:00 is the Sandy River delta, the largest along the Columbia in Oregon, it has diverted the main stream 2 miles north. It has a number of distributary channels, occupied during flood water. (0.2)

22.9   Passing Lewis and Clark Park. Note Troutdale silts in bluff. (0.3)

23.2   Stop sign. Bridge to Troutdale on right. Keep left. Entering Scenic Highway. (1.2)

24.4   Highway cuts exposed gravels and sands of the Troutdale formation. (1.1)

25.5   STOP, across from cliffs before reaching bridge. Big Bend of the Sandy River, an incised meander. Here are some of the best exposures of Troutdale gravels. Note steep foreset bedding and channel-cutting at base of conglomerate beds just east of Bridge. Quartzite pebbles can be found in the conglomerates, which were probably derived from the Precambrian rocks of British Columbia. (0.2)

25.7   Upper Sandy River Bridge, keep straight ahead. (0.3)

26.0   Dabney State Park. Note incised meanders and terraces at several levels along the Sandy. (0.3)

Historical photograph (1920?) of the logged-off Gorge, with Crown Point in the upper right. Rooster Rock landslide block and fish cannery in the lower part of the picture. (Historical Society photo)

26.3   Milepost 5 and junction. (0.7)

27.0   Entering Springdale (on the 200-foot terrace). (0.3)

27.3   Springdale junction. Keep right. (0.1)

27.4   Sandy River Road Jct., Keep left. We have been rising up several terraces to the summit surface, which is at 600 feet west of Corbett, and continues to rise east of Corbett at about 100 feet to the mile. (0.8)

28.2   Road junction. Keep to the left. (1.0)

29.2   Milepost 8. (0.3)

29.5   Entering Corbett. Just north of this point on the Freeway I-80 below, the top of the Yakima Basalt rises above river level on the east flank of the Willamette syncline. It also crops out at one point in the bed of the Sandy River about 3 miles south of this point. The summit surface here is largely constructional, representing the surface of the Troutdale, covered here and there by Boring lavas, but only eroded to the stage of late youth. (0.4)

29.9   Road to the left returns to Freeway below. Now on the summit level at about 800 feet elevation. (0.3)

30.2   Milepost 9. (1.3)

31.4   STOP at Chanticleer Lookout (Women's Forum State Park), 850 feet elevation. Excellent view up Gorge across landslide amphitheatre in the foreground. Taking the Vista House on Crown Point as 12:00, Beacon Rock plug lies directly above; Mount Pleasant and Mount Zion Boring volcanoes lie across the river at 10:45 and 11:15. Rooster Rock landslide block is at river level, 11:00; Phoca Rock (named for the harbor seal *Phoca vitulina*) in the river at 11:50; Larch Mountain shield volcano is on the skyline at 1:00, and Pepper Mountain lies below at 1:10. Beneath Crown Point, the contact of the southdipping Yakima Basalt with the overlying Troutdale may be easily seen. Road cuts along the highway just west of Crown Point are in Troutdale, overlain by a 50-feet flow of Boring lava from Ross Mountain volcano. This contact may be seen from 1:00 to 2:00. (0.4)

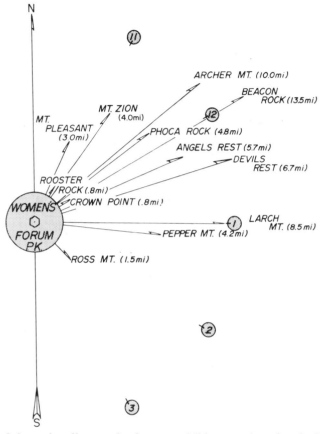

Orientation diagram for features visible on a clear day, looking up the Columbia River Gorge from Chanticleer Viewpoint (Women's Forum Park). Boxing the compass, the features can be identified as follows:

10:45 Mount Pleasant, a Boring Lava cinder cone.

11:00 Rooster Rock, a landslide block of Yakima Basalt.

11:15 Mount Zion, a Boring Lava cinder cone.

11:45 Archer Mountain, a peak capped with a flow of Yakima Basalt.

11:50 Phoca Rock, probably another landslide block of Yakima Basalt.

12:00 Crown Point, underlain by Wanapum Basalt, capped with Troutdale Formation.

12:00 Beacon Rock, a volcanic plug or neck.

12:15 Angel's Rest, a promontory of Cascade Lava.

12:25 Devil's Rest, the same.

 1:00 Larch Mountain, a Cascade Lava shield volcano.

 1:10 Pepper Mountain, a Boring Lava cinder cone.

 1:20 Ross Mountain, the same.

31.8   Junction, keep left. Larch Mountain road to right goes
thirteen miles on a good paved road to the glaciated
summit, with a lookout at 4056 feet elevation. The western larch does *not* grow on Larch Mountain. Early lum-
bermen called th noble fir (*Abies nobilis*) larch. (0.3)

32.1   STOP. Highway drop off here is due to continuing
landsliding. Baked red contact of Boring flow from Ross
Mt. volcano (1 m S.E.) lying above Troutdale gravels.
Gravels between here and Crown Point contain large
amounts of volcaniclastic material, steeply southwest-
dipping foreset bedding, large anomalous boulders in
finer matrix, and poor sorting. (0.5)

32.6   Optional STOP. Crown Point Vista House, rest rooms
and sales counter. Elevation 720 feet. Note across river
to the north the gently west-sloping surface of Troutdale, capped by Mount Pleasant and Mount Zion volcanoes. (0.1)

32.7   Troutdale conglomerate outcrops along road on right.
(0.4)

33.1   Pillow lavas in uppermost flow of Yakima Basalt lying
in channel above "brickbat" jointed basalt. *"Pillows"*
are formed when basalt flows into water, so there must
have been a river or lake here. (0.4)

33.5   Entering the famous "Figure Eight Loops" of the old
scenic Gorge highway. This highway was finished in
1916 and was then considered a remarkable feat of highway engineering. It displays the best example of a western Oregon rain-forest that you will see in the Gorge,
without leaving your car. (1.4)

34.9   Optional STOP after crossing bridge. Latourell Falls,
249 feet. Named from a pioneer settler in the locality.
Talbot State Park was donated to the State in 1929
by the lumber baron, Guy W. Talbot. Note that the
falls pour over a single flow of brickbat basalt with
curved columns toward the base, (entablature and colonnade) and that the recent notch at the top is only
20 feet deep. (0.3)

35.2   Milepost 14. (0.9)

36.1   Shepperds Dell. Falls can be seen by looking back at
5:00. (0.1)

Hercules Pillars, looking west down-river from near Bridal Veil. Most of these erosional remnants of the entablature of a massive flow of Yakima Basalt were removed during freeway construction. Crown Point can be seen to the left of the lone tree (Historical Society photo)

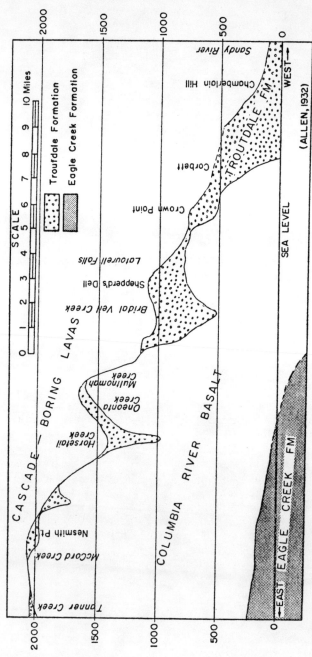

Section of the west part of the Gorge between the Sandy River and Tanner Creek, showing elevations of the contacts between the formations exposed. The Eagle Creek-Yakima Basalt contact comes above river level east of Oneonta Creek, and rises eastward at about 30 feet per mile. The upper contact of the Yakima Basalt is irregular, suggesting valleys up to 600 feet deep, filled with Troutdale gravels. The average eastward rise of the Troutdale Formation is 2000 feet in 22 miles, or 90 feet per mile.

36.2   Milepost 15. Brickbat basalt (entablature) overlying basal columnar basalt (colonnade) forms "mushroom" effect along highway. (0.9)

37.1   Milepost 16. Crossing Bridal Veil Creek. Falls are *below* the bridge, and may be seen by looking back towards 7:00 after crossing bridge. The section of Troutdale exposed in the creek bed above extends from 500' to over 1000' el., the thickest section found in the Gorge. Cape Horn lies across river at 9:00. (0.7)

37.8   Bridal Veil junction to freeway. Keep right. Cape Horn at 8:00 to 9:00. Lower part of cliff is Yakima Basalt, upper part Troutdale formation, capped by lava from Mt. Zion volcano. (0.4)

38.2   Milepost 17. (0.1)

38.3   For the next mile or so, look up through the trees on the right to the basalt cliffs at head of 500-foot talus slopes. Western pinnacle (elevation 1600 feet) is called Angels Rest; eastern summit (2400 feet) Devils Rest. Here the base of Troutdale formation lies at 965 feet, and top of formation is at 1000 feet. (1.8)

40.1   Milepost 19. (0.2)

40.3   Wahkeena Falls. Is said to be a Yakima Indian word meaning "most beautiful", and the falls lives up to its name. A multiple fall, 242 feet high. Trail leads ½ mile to main falls. (0.6)

40.8   STOP. Multnomah Falls, dropping down over 400 feet from a typical "hanging valley", is the best-known falls in the Gorge, and the highest. On April 9, 1806, Meriwether Lewis wrote:
            "We passed several beautiful cascades which fell from a great height over the stupendious rocks which closes the river on both sides nearly ... the most remarkable of these cascades falls about 300 feet perpendicularly over a solid rock into a narrow bottom of the river on the south side"
        You should examine the rocks in the walls of the Lodge. Yakima black basalt, Cascade or Boring gray basalt, Troutdale quartzite boulders and Eagle Creek petrified and opalized wood may all be identified. Be sure to visit

Multnomah Falls drops over 5 flows of Yakima Basalt; those visible, from top to bottom, are:

6. 20' of the collonade of an 80-foot thick flow, notched by Multnomah Creek.

5. 75' of pillow lava, which came out under water.

4. 35' of a thin glassy flow, with well-formed entablature and collonade.

3. 120', consisting of two tiers of hackly-jointed basalt, with no collonade.

2. 140', topped by a vesicular zone which forms a notch; entablature with thin columns, collonade has 2 to 4-foot columns.

1. 70' of entablature beneath the lower falls.

The total height of the falls by this measurement (Waters, 1973), is 460 feet, not the 640 usually cited!

(Ore. Dept. of Transp. photo)

the Forest Service Information Center, where an excellent geological exhibit may be seen. The main Multnomah Falls is said to be 541 feet high, the lower falls 69 feet, with a drop of 10 feet in the cascades between; in all 620 feet. The main falls drops across three basalt flows, a fourth causes the lower falls. The top of the Troutdale in the cliffs above is at 1600 feet elevation (see page 88). Multnomah is an Indian tribal name, first used by Lewis and Clark in their journals for November 3, 1805, as "Mulknoma," applied to the river now called the Willamette. They later applied it to a tribe on the Columbia. Ethnologists believe it originally meant "down river." (0.3)

41.1   Milepost 20. (0.3)

41.4   Note landslide scar above at 3:00 and debris in river around navigation tower at 9:00. In 1946, when the freeway below was first under construction, talus from a borrow pit was used for road metal by the Highway Department. Springs rains caused a landslide which carried down an estimated 300,000 cubic yards of material, the talus breaking away for 1000 feet up to the bedrock cliffs above, temporarily blocking the highway and the railroad. The navigation marker now visible in the river was raised 20 feet out of the water and tilted 30° by the uplifted toe of the slide. (0.6)

42.0   Milepost 21. (1.0)

43.0   STOP, Oneonta Gorge. Turn off right and park on or beyond old bridge. This youthful gorge is cut in two flows of basalt, each nearly 100 feet thick. A few feet above highway level is the contact with still another flow below. Along this contact which drops to near and below creek level as one goes upstream the 900 feet to the falls, the writer mapped sixty five holes, from 6 inches to 3 feet in diameter, representing molds of trees overwhelmed by the upper flow. Most of the holes extend generally east and west. In some of them, remnants of carbonized, opalized and otherwise silicified wood which once constituted the tree material could be found. The word Oneonta is of New York origin, but for nearly 20 years before 1887, a sidewheel river steamboat named "Oneonta" plied the river, and it is possible that the creek derived its name from some incident connected with the boat. (0.3)

43.3   Horsetail Falls. 221 feet, apparently over one flow. The underlying Eagle Creek formation, although not exposed on the south side here, probably lies beneath the talus and debris above river level from this point on for the next 15 miles. Notice the retreat of the cliffs towards the south in the next mile, and the development of an alluvial or talus fan over a mile wide. Notice also the retreat of the cliffs on the north side of the Gorge. Archer Mountain, at 8:00 and the gently west-sloping Fletcher Flat west of it, are only small remnants of basalt extending northwards for less than 3 miles. (0.5)

43.8   Ainsworth State Park. The best developed pinnacles in Yakima Basalt occur along the southern cliffs for the next 3 miles. St. Peters Dome (page 9) should be visible as a symmetrical tower 1500 feet above river level. If the day is clear, it is possible to see the thin flows of Cascade andesite forming the upper cliffs above the contact which lies at about 1800 feet. More than 100 feet of Troutdale was found by the writer behind St. Peters Dome and in a ridge to the east, Nesmith Point. The upper cliffs of Nesmith Point exhibit a cross-section of one of the Cascade volcanoes, with vent exposed. (1.2)

45.0   Junction of Scenic Highway with Freeway, I-80N, near Dodson, keep right. The Cascade summit surface in Benson Plateau south of here lies at elevations from 3,900 to 4,300 feet, and numerous small cirques have been cut by ice on the east sides of the plateau, ridge crests and volcanic cones, at elevations above 3500 feet. (0.5)

45.5   Milepost 36. Beacon Rock, named by Lewis and Clark in 1806, lies across the river at 9:00. It has been called the eroded vent-filling of a Pliocene volcano, standing 840 feet above the river. It is actually the southernmost of several necks (or a great north-south dike) extending to the north for more than 2 miles. It is red, scoriaceous, and vesicular near the summit. Baked contacts with Eagle Creek are found to the south and southwest, and the columnar structure on the east side is horizontal, east and west. On the west side the columns are vertical.

At 10:00 the basalt capping of Hamilton Mountain rests on Eagle Creek at an elevation of 1550 feet. The basalt rises steeply to the north for 2 miles, where it pinches out at about 3000 feet. (1.8)

". . . a remarkable high detached rock Stands in a bottom on the Star. Side . . . about 800 feet high and 400 paces around we call the Beacon rock." (Lewis and Clark, October 31st, 1805). (Oregon Dept. of Transp. photo)

Looking northeast across head of Cascade Landslide. A. Mount Rainier, B. Mount Adams, C. Ridge of Ohanape- cosh Formation, the oldest rocks in the Gorge, D. Green- leaf Peak, a thin cap of Yakima Basalt over light-colored Eagle Creek Formation, E. Table Mountain, capped by at least six flows of Yakima Basalt, F. Aldrich Butte, com- posed of Eagle Creek Formation. (Delano photo)

Looking east across Bonneville Dam and the lower end of the Cascade Landslide, which came down from the left 700 years ago to dam the river, divert it a mile to the south, and probably give rise to the legend of the "Bridge of the Gods". A. Dog Mountain, B. Wind Mountain, C. Carson intracanyon flow, D. Cascade Landslide, E - E. Old course of river. (Delano photo)

47.3   Bridge across McCord Creek; Elowah Falls through
        trees at 3:00. The road cuts exhibits the first good out-
        crops along the highway of the Eagle Creek formation
        on the south side of the Gorge. Beneath Elowah Falls,
        the contact of basalt over Eagle Creek is exposed at
        an elevation of 220 feet. These falls have a vertical drop
        of 289 feet, the lower part of the cliff being undercut
        in the soft pebbly tuffaceous Eagle Creek. The basal
        columnar portion (collonade) of the flow is well exhibit-
        ed here. A few steps east of the highway bridge a vertical
        trunk of petrified wood 2½ feet in diameter once stood
        just above highway level. When the Scenic Highway
        was built in 1915, this tree stood nearly 10 feet high
        in the face of the road cut (Williams, 1916). Vandal ero-
        sion had reduced it to 3 feet when the highway depart-
        ment took it out at the time the freeway was built.
        Note the poor sorting of the mud-flow debris in which
        it was enclosed (0.2).

47.5   Milepost 38. Good exposures of Eagle Creek formation
        beginning to appear, dipping 5° to the southwest (appar-
        ent dip horizontal). (1.0)

48.5   Milepost 39. Moffett Creek bridge. Joseph LeConte
        (1874) collected fossil leaves from a carbonaceous layer
        beneath the west abutment of the railroad bridge in
        1871 and 1873. J.S. Diller collected leaves here (1896)
        which were determined to be Miocene in age (0.9)

49.4   Entering best exposures of Eagle Creek along highway,
        which dip 6 to 9° to the southeast. Fragments of petri-
        fied wood not uncommon in these exposures. (0.2)

49.6   Exit to Bonneville Dam and fish ladders. Bonneville
        Dam visible at 11:00, Fish Hatchery at 10:00, with Table
        Mountain above it across the river (at the head of the
        great Bonneville or Cascade landslide), where basalt
        overlies Eagle Creek at 2300 feet elevation. Four miles
        south up Tanner Creek on the west wall, Troutdale ex-
        posures appear between the Cascade andesites and Yak-
        ima Basalt at 1950 to 2100 feet elevation. (0.4)

50.0   The highway here on left is cut in Bonney Rock, a great
        compound feederdike of diabase, upon which the south
        end of Bonneville Dam is based. (0.6)

Tooth Rock Tunnel was drilled through a landslide block of Yakima Basalt. This picture was taken before construction of the west-bound freeway bridge across the face of the rock. The shoreline on the left consists of Cascade Landslide. (Ore. Dept. of Transp. photo)

50.6   Tunnel at Tooth Rock in landslide block of Yakima
        Basalt; rock was historically one of the major barriers
        to early travel. Note large area of landslide across the
        river, extending 3 miles back from river to base of Table
        Mountain. River has been shoved south nearly 1½ miles
        from its straight course here, to form the Cascades of
        the Columbia before the construction of Bonneville
        Dam. The surface of this landslide exhibits undrained
        depression, and tilted trees, as evidence of the recency
        of movement which has been dated at about 1260 A.D.
        (0.3)

50.9   Exit to Eagle Creek Park and Eagle Creek bridge. The
        elevation of top of Eagle Creek formation is at nearly
        500 feet, two miles up Eagle Creek it is 400 feet. On
        right is the Cascade salmon hatchery. (0.8)

51.7   Note irregularities of structure and composition of
        Eagle Creek formation due to landsliding known as the
        "Ruckel slide". (0.6)

52.3   "Bridge of the Gods" at 10:00. This bridge connects the
        upper end of the Cascade landslide with the south shore,
        and formerly spanned part of the Cascades of the Co-
        lumbia, now ponded by dam waters. (0.5)

52.8   Exit to Cascade Locks and to interstate bridge. Contin-
        ue on freeway, unless you wish to cross and return via
        Vancouver (see page 127). Note widening of the Gorge
        on both sides of the river. Just east of Cascade Locks,
        the Eagle Creek contact rises to its maximum elevation
        of 620 feet in Herman Creek. The high Benson Plateau
        to the south has a summit elevation of 4200 feet; be-
        neath the thousand-foot andesite capping, from 2500 to
        3100 feet lies a bed of cinders, red ash, and volcanic
        bombs believed to be correlative with the Rhododen-
        dron Formation. (1.2)

54.0   STOP. Cascade Locks lava flow. Spectacular exhibit on
        both sides of highway of columnar jointing in zeolitized
        porphyritic andesite; showing fan-structure of columns
        at right angles to surface of flow. Less well-defined cross-
        jointing is also visible. The lava is diktytaxitic, slightly
        vesicular. (1.7)

55.7   Approaching Herman Creek Bridge. Government Island
        (jetty-rock quarry) and 4 other erosion remnants occur-

ring to the left of the highway in the next mile are dissimilar in composition from other intrusives in the Eagle Creek formation, being uniform holocrystalline pyroxene trachyte. (0.8)

56.5   Milepost 47. (0.6)

57.1   On the right of the highway for the next 3 miles is a narrow but flat-topped ridge which has diverted Herman Creek to the west for a mile and a half. The lower part (below 400' el.) is a south-side remnant of intracanyon lava from Wind River channel in Washington. The upper and older, reaching an elevation of 1000 feet, had a local source. The surface of the lower flow as it debouches from Wind River Valley may be seen at 10:00. Wind River has cut a vertical-walled narrow canyon 300 feet deep in the flow. The Columbia river was undoubtedly dammed for a time. (0.9)

58.0   This is an area of active landsliding, which has repeatedly disturbed the highway roadbed, lifting it up tens of feet. Removal of millions of yards by the highway engineers has failed to stop the movement. (0.6)

58.6   Good view at 11:00 of the flat top of the Wind River intracanyon flow, which came from a small volcano, Trout Creek Hill, 15 miles up the valley to the northwest. (0.5)

59.1   Due south of here, the highest exposure of Troutdale gravels in the Gorge were found by the writer at an elevation of 2700 feet, also the highest elevation reached by the Yakima Basalt in the south wall of the Gorge. (0.3)

59.4   Optional STOP. Exposures along the highway of Wind River intracanyon olivine basalt. (1.1)

60.5   Wind Mountain at 10:00 and Shellrock Mountain at 12:00 on the skyline. These "twin guardians of the Columbia", rising to nearly 2000 feet on either side of the river, are both similar in composition, being fine-grained, intrusive granodiorite-porphyry, with predominantly labradorite phenocrysts but with dominant oligoclase-andesine in the groundmass. Baked contacts with Eagle Creek were found on both sides of the river. In the saddle south of Shellrock Mountain, xenoliths of basalt in

Wind Mountain intrusion (grano diorite), with Dog Mountain (Yakima Basalt) in background; separated by a fault and by a landslide area more than a mile wide and extending north three miles from the river. The 8-degree slope of its moving surface can be seen in the picture. (Ore. Dept. of Transp. photo)

the granodiorite, and a baked, amygdule-filled basalt breccia was found, indicating the post-Yakima Basalt age of the intrusives. Similar circular bodies of about the same areal extent (1 square mile) were found 2, 4, and 6 miles north of Wind Mountain, indicating a line of central intrusives lying on the Mount Defiance-Mount Hood axis. The writer believes that the river followed a consequent course around the northern edge of the Pliocene lavas, and was superimposed across the underlying intrusives, which possibly never built up any extrusive volcanic edifices. (1.1)

61.6   Approaching Gorton Creek bridge at Wyeth exit. (0.7)

62.3   When the freeway was first built, the road cut here showed the easternmost exposure of Eagle Creek formation, baked to a brick-red by the nearby Shellrock intrusive. The tuff was changed to a brittle red jaspery material, the pebbles of the conglomerate were sheared and contorted. (0.5)

62.8   West edge of Shellrock Mountain. The angle of repose of the "shell rock" talus slopes is about 42°. Ripley once stated that Shellrock Mountain "rested upon ice". Origin of this idea was from the gusts of icy wind which come out of the talus during the summer months, obviously derived from snow which has filtered down into the loose talus during the winter months. Mount Defiance, 2 miles south of Shellrock Mountain, is the highest peak, after Mount Hood, in the entire Gorge area, reaching 4960 feet. Like Larch Mountain to the west, it is one of the later (Pleistocene) volcanoes and still retains much of its shield-like surface. One flow from Mt. Defiance is recent enough to have come down the wall of the Gorge to the 1000 foot elevation.

Across the river at 11:00, Dog Mountain and its northern extension, Auspurger Mountain, rise to 2989 and 3684 feet. This block is the easternmost isolated area of Yakima Basalt on the north side. The folded lavas go below river level, but only extend 4 miles north, where the contact with underlying Ohanapecosh is at 2500 feet elevation. (0.8)

63.6   Optional STOP, just beyond bridge at east fault contact of Shellrock intrusion. Milepost 53. Yakima Basalt at river level. The narrow canyon to the south and the shearing and fracturing of the basalt and abundance of agate in vesicles and fractures in the cliff face, establishes the location of the fault contact with the Shellrock intrusive. The east side of this fault has been dropped down at least 500 feet. (0.4)

64.0   Lindsey Creek bridge. The upper contact of Yakima Basalt in the creek bed 2 miles south lies at 2300 feet. The Dog Mountain basalt mass across the river forms a south-plunging anticline, faulted at the west side of the mountain (note westward dips of 11 to 15° on the west side of Dog Creek, and eastward dips on the east side of Dog Creek). (1.6)

65.6   Exit to Starvation Creek and picnic ground. Notice fine columnar colonnade in Yakima Basalt at base of entablature cliff. Named by occupants of a train stalled here by snow slides for 4 days in 1884. The falls, cascading down 186 feet, are the easternmost of the spectacular series in the Gorge. The Dog Mountain anticline is visible across the river at 10:00. (0.8)

66.4   Viento Creek Park exit. Although Viento is Spanish for windy, and this region is the windiest in the Gorge, the name has an entirely different origin, derived from the first two letters of the names of three railroad men, Henry Villard, William Endicott, and Tolman. Williams (1916) reports 500 feet of Troutdale gravels in Viento Creek between 2000 and 2500 feet elevation. This is an unusual thickness, approaching the thickness at Bridal Veil. (1.1)

67.5   Note horizontal intracayon lavas across river at 10:00. This is the Little White Salmon flow, which has come 20 miles down the valley to the Columbia, where it once dammed the river to an elevation of 500 plus feet. (0.7)

68.2   Perham Creek. Mitchell Point, ahead, is Yakima Basalt dipping 30° to the southeast, capped by 100 feet of Troutdale-type quartzitic gravels, and unconformably overlain by later lavas with low initial dip. Across the river at 10:00-11:00 lies the Underwood Mountain shield volcano, whose intracanyon lavas unconformably overlie steeply east-dipping Yakima Basalt a few hundred feet above the river level. Underwood lavas crossed and probably dammed the river, remnants crop out for 2 miles east of Mitchell Point. (1.1)

69.3   Passing Mitchell Point, one of the windiest spots in the
        Gorge. The old Scenic Highway tunneled through the
        point, 50 feet above the present freeway. (1.8)

71.1   East-dipping bright yellow palagonite tuff and breccia
        of Ruthton Point, the result of lava from a nearby intra-
        canyon volcano or possibly from Underwood volcano
        across the river, pouring into a lake formed by a lava
        dam. (0.2)

71.3   Intracanyon lava in road cuts, have been cemented to
        contain groundwater. (0.1)

71.4   First Hood River exit 62. Entering Hood River Valley
        and syncline, which extends for 20 miles to the south
        with average width of 5 miles. The east wall of the valley
        is a fault escarpment, with a vertical displacement of
        over 2000 feet. Abundant glacial till and outwash
        occupies the valley bottom, exposed in road cuts and
        in the youthful canyon of the river, incised 200 to 300
        feet below the valley surface. If the day is clear it is
        possible to catch a glimpse of Mt. Adams at 9:00. (1.5)

72.9   Second Hood River exit. Since passing Mitchell Point,
        note the beginning of a sharp change in vegetation, dic-
        tated by the Cascade Mountains rain shadow. Douglas
        fir and hemlock have given way to deciduous trees and
        live oak. The annual rainfall at Hood River is less than
        30 inches, as compared with over 40 inches at Portland.
        (0.3)

73.2   Milepost 64. Bridge across Hood River. Thick quartzitic
        gravels (Dalles-Troutdale) rest upon west-dipping ba-
        salt at the east approach to the upper bridge south of
        this point. We have just passed the axis of the Hood
        River-White Salmon River syncline. (0.3)

73.5   Exit 64 to Toll bridge across river to north side high-
        way and to Mt. Hood. Keep straight on, unless you wish
        to cross and return to Vancouver. Quarries on the right
        in Yakima Basalt, thoroughly shattered adjacent to
        fault zone. Note west-dipping basalts across river, as
        we move into the Bingen anticline. (0.5)

74.0   Approaching the axis of the Bingen anticline to be seen
        across river at 10:00. (1.0)

Looking down-river across the Mosier syncline towards the Bingen anticline. Mitchell Point in center of view. Note Bretz flood highwater line at 1000 feet elevation (-X-) in upper right. (Oregon Dept. of Transp. photo)

The Rowena Loops and Mayer State Park viewpoint on the Scenic Highway east of Mosier. Bretz floodwaters topped this mesa-like bench, and stripped off most of The Dalles Formation which originally covered it. A remnant patch can be seen near the top of the picture across the river in the center of the Mosier syncline. (Sam Sargent photo)

75.0   Columnar Yakima Basalt colonnades in cliffs at 3:00.
        Dalles Formation gravels, similar in age to the Trout-
        dale, are found on the east side of Bingen anticline to
        the south at 2400 feet elevation. (0.9)

75.9   Milepost 67. The axis of the Mosier syncline trends
        northeast up the Columbia River at 11:00. The base
        of The Dalles beds in the center of the syncline a mile
        southwest of Mosier is at about 750 feet. (0.5)

76.4   The fences along the railroad track are designed to auto-
        matically set the railroad block signals in case large
        boulders break through to the tracks. (2.1)

78.5   Approaching town of Mosier. Synclinal axis at 10:00.
        (0.3)

78.8   Mosier exit 69 and overpass. Take exit for 9-mile sce-
        nic loop. Crossing axis of syncline. (0.3)

79.2   Note scabland surfaces on dip-slope of basalt across
        river up to elevations of about 900 feet. (0.4)

80.5   Note remnants of Dalles beds and high gravel bars from
        12:00 to 3:00 particularly on hill at 1:00. Floodwaters
        must have covered this wide grassed area, depositing
        debris in lee of spur to the east. (0.9)

81.4   Milepost 70. Leaving axis of Mosier syncline, which now
        lies across river. Structural terraces on basalt flows
        across river were scoured out by Bretz floodwaters to
        an elevation of over 900 feet. (0.4)

81.8   Exit to Rest Area. (2.2)

84.0   Milepost 75. Note high Bretz flood bar with gravel pit
        at 9:30, east of Klickitat above town of Lyle. (1.5)

85.5   Mayer Park and Rowena Exit 76. (1.1)

86.6   Approaching axis of Ortley anticline across river at 9:30.
        Flows thinned and folded to form vertical hogbacks, and
        down-dropped on west side. Axis of anticline about ½
        mile east of hogbacks. Note number of flows (at least
        15) in cliffs at 9:00 (1.0)

At least six flows of Yakima Basalt, stripped of soil and cliffed by the Spokane floods just east of Lyle. For geology buffs, the uppermost flow is the *Pomona Basalt Member* of the Saddle Mountains Basalt Formation, and the lower five flows belong to the *Priest Rapids Basalt Member* of the Wanapum Basalt Formation. (Oregon Department of Transp. photo)

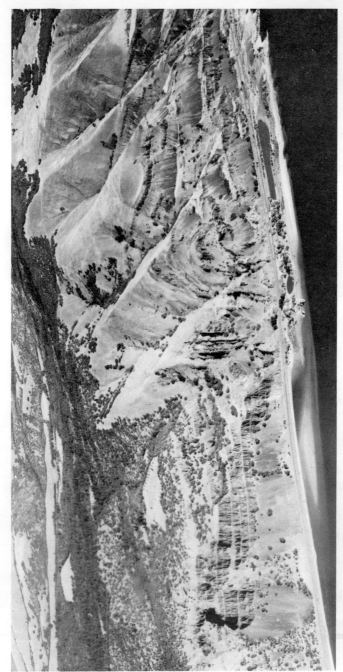

Looking northeast, with the Ortley (Columbia Hills) anticline on the right. The abruptly bent and broken western flank of the fold, with the flows of the Yakima Basalt standing vertically appears in the foreground (Sam Sargent photo)

87.6   Axis of Ortley anticline at 9:00. Dalles beds have been stripped off crest of anticline to the south. Entering Dalles syncline, originally filled with Dalles beds to an elevation of over 1000 feet, which south-ward, rise to 2000 feet. Still farther southwestward they can be traced to an elevation of over 3000 feet before they are covered by Cascade lavas. (1.7)

89.3   Top of ridge below Crites Point. Entering The Dalles scabland area. Note patch of high depositional terraces in reentrant across river at 8:00. (0.2)

89.5   Quarry in high flood gravel bar on left of highway. (1.0)

90.5   Scablands on both sides of highway. (0.5)

91.0   Exit 82, first of The Dalles exits. The name (from the French word meaning "flagstone gutter") was first used in Oregon by Gabriel Franchere, in his 1814 narrative describing the Long Narrows of the river here. Cliffs

Bretz Flood deposits form a series of terraces in a reentrant high above the river five miles north of The Dalles (Sam Sargent photo)

from 12:00 to 3:00 in The Dalles formation, first described by Thomas Condon (1874) as a remnant of an old lake bed. These beds have been dated on the basis of vertebrate fossils as Pliocene age, equivalent to the Troutdale. (4.6)

95.6   Take Exit 87 to Interstate bridge Junction. (0.3)

95.9   Stop Sign. Turn left to Interstate bridge and cross the Columbia River for return trip to Vancouver via the north side; or else turn right ¼ mile to see pillow lavas in Yakima Basalt at highway junction.

Yakima Basalt pillows in subaqueous flow at junction with Highway 197 (south of freeway overpass to interstate bridge) east of The Dalles. Note elongation of the pillows, with dips to the right, indicators of the direction of flow. Light-colored matrix between pillows is finely divided volcanic glass, known as "palagonite", a result of the chill-shock when liquid lava meets water (Sam Sargent photo)

CHAPTER 3
GEOLOGIC ROAD LOG:

The Dalles Junction to Vancouver
via Highways U.S. 197
and Washington 14

by
John Eliot Allen and Paul E. Hammond

0.0   From bridge junction of highway I-80N, turn north on
       U.S. 197 and cross toll free interstate bridge to Washing-
       ton. Completion of the 8,700 foot long The Dalles Dam
       in 1960 drowned the historic "dalles of the Columbia",
       a series of deep gutters where the river actually stood
       on edge, and where prehistoric indian tribes had fished
       for millenia. The present lake extends 25 miles east to
       the John Day Dam, with a pool level 160 feet above
       sea level. Information on the dam and the surrounding
       area is described in a display at the viewpoint to be
       visited at mile 1.2. The dam rests on the Wanapum Ba-
       salt member of the Yakima Group, within the broad
       trough of The Dalles syncline. When crossing the
       bridge, at 1:00 in the river bank is a north-trending fault
       (west side down about 40 feet) exposed between the
       bridge and the lock canal. (1.0)

1.0   Continue ahead. Road junction on left goes to Dal-
       lesport and municipal airport, built on a plain underlain
       by Bretz flood gravels. (0.1)

1.1   Turn right at road junction to The Dalles Dam view-
       point. Recent sand dunes along the road mantle the
       lee slopes of scabland mounds. (0.1)

1.2   STOP. The viewpoint and Visitors Center lies upon the
       intersection of the fault seen from the bridge and the
       axis (lowest point) of The Dalles syncline. The road to
       the viewpoint follows the scoured-out fault zone. The

skyline ridge to the north is the Ortley-Columbia Hills
anticline; Signal Hill, above the dam across the river
is capped by The Dalles Formation, which also caps
the entire skyline to the south and southwest, and forms
the prominent bluff behind the city. Mount Hood can
be seen on a clear day, 30 miles to the southwest. Upon
leaving the viewpoint, you will be passing for the next
5 miles through the best example of scablands to be
seen on the trip. The Bretz flood of 13,000 years ago
swept across the Big Bend of the Columbia ripping out
The Dalles Formation which filled the syncline, and

"Long Narrows" and Celilo Canal just east of The Dalles
Dam (under construction in the distance at time of photograph). This flood-scoured scabland vista is now submerged beneath the ponded waters. The former Indian fishing grounds can be seen in the extreme lower left. (Sam
Sargent photo)

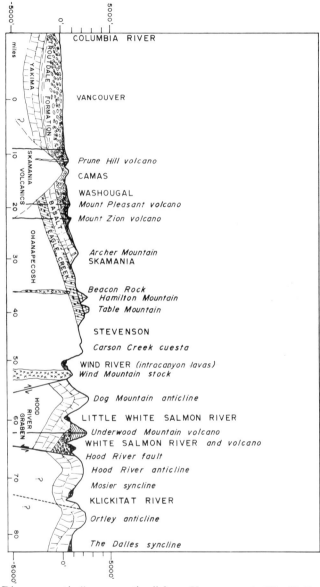

Diagrammatic "cross-section" from Vancouver to The Dalles along the north side of the Gorge, showing the relative positions and attitudes of the geologic formations. Note that the vertical scale is exaggerated about 10 times. A similar sketch of the south side of the Gorge is on page 78. Towns and rivers are identified by large capital letters, geologic formations by small capital letters, mountains and structures are in italics.

tearing out the basalt columns and blocks, especially along fracture zones of weakness, to produce the characteristic elongated little tablelands, separated by, now undrained, channels. Over 800 feet deep, the flood waters travelled at perhaps 30 or 40 miles per hour! (0.1)

1.3   Return to highway junction and turn right. Note that the flood scoured off the slopes of the Columbia Hills up to about 1000 feet. Above this line there are no outcrops of basalt, and the slopes are smooth, veneered with soil and wind-blown silt. (2.4)

3.7   Turn left (west) at junction onto Washington highway 14. The small hill across the river at 11:30 is Wetle Butte, a minor anticline within the larger syncline; the high ridge above, where the high-water mark of the flood is outlined by vegetation, is Sevenmile Hill, the southeast flank of the Ortley anticline. (1.3)

5.0   Continue ahead past junction on left with Dallesport road. (0.4)

5.4   At 2:00 high in the slopes above, the Bretz flood highwater marks, a series of little gravel terraces can be seen in a reentrant. (0.9)

6.3   Entering the eastern end of the watergap through the Ortley-Columbia Hills anticline. The roadcuts are in southeast-dipping flows of the lower Wanapum Basalt and Grande Ronde Basalt of the Yakima Group. (0.2)

6.5   The number 0 16 painted on the rock in the road cut marks the lowest flow of Wanapum Basalt. (0.2)

6.7   The top flow of the Grande Ronde Basalt is marked 0 15. For the next 2 miles, the dipping flows are marked

Airview looking northwest from above The Dalles (lower left), across the Big Bend of the Columbia River. Mount Rainier may be seen to the right of Mount Adams in the upper right. The river crosses the Ortley anticline in the middle of the picture, turns left down the axis of the Mosier syncline. Low bluffs above The Dalles on the left are composed of The Dalles Formation. Note the horizontal line at 1000 feet elevation (Bretz flood highwater mark) across the flank of Seven-Mile Hill on the left. (Oregon Department of Transp. photo)

in descending order. As we go farther into the anticline, the dips change from 22 degrees to horizontal as the axis of the fold is reached. (1.7)

8.4   The lowest flows of the Grande Ronde Basalt are marked 0 3 to 0 1 in the road cuts as we cross the anticlinal axis. Across the river in the face of Sevenmile Hill the whole fold can be seen. (0.2)

8.6   West dipping flow 0 4 of Grande Ronde Basalt exposed in roadcut. (0.5)

9.1   STOP. This is the site of one of the most spectacular geologic structures in the upper Gorge. Through here passes the Rowena Gap fault, which breaks the northwest flank of the Ortley anticline, and forms a series of vertical hogbacks in the cliffs above. The 600 to 1000 foot movement on the fault has dropped down Wanapum Basalt on the west against Grande Ronde Basalt on the east. At least four lava flows have been dragged up into a vertical position, shattered, squeezed out and thinned by the movement. Note the abundance of finely broken basalt in the road cuts. This basalt breccia forms a 300 foot wide zone along the highway. The

Looking west at the east flank of the Ortley anticline just northwest of The Dalles. The Yakima Basalt is dipping towards the camera. The Bretz flood highwater line cuts across the middle of the picture (-X-), below this line all soil was stripped away, and little vegetation can flourish. (Sam Sargent photo)

fault dies out upwards, as well as to the west across the river (just east of Mayer Park Lookout) into a sharp fold. A broad bench high up on the northwest is underlain by a very young flow of Yakima Basalt, known in central Washington as the Pomona Flow. (1.5)

10.6   Tunnel in Wanapum Basalt. (0.4)

11.0   Town of Lyle. Visible in a quarry face above are foreset-bedded Bretz flood and older gravels more than 100 feet thick, which underlie the 300 foot bench overlooking the town. (0.2)

11.2   Junction with highway 142, leading north up Klickitat River to Goldendale and Glenwood. Continue ahead. (0.1)

11.3   Bridge over Klickitat River, which drains much of the area around Mount Adams volcano. (0.1)

Vertical ridges formed by Yakima Basalt lava flows that have been crushed, thinned and squeezed out, and tilted 90 degrees on the west flank of the Ortley anticline. (Sam Sargent photo)

11.4   Junction with Balch Lake Road (old highway). A mile
        up this side road thick flood gravels with foreset beds
        dipping north up the canyon are exposed in road cuts.
        A mile farther on, Balch Lake lies at 600 feet elevation
        in a Bretz flood channel cut in The Dalles Formation.
        This possible side trip rejoins the main road at mile
        16.2. Proceeding west, the highway roadcuts expose
        Wanapum Basalt. (1.4)

12.8   The highway climbs up through the *Roza Member* of
        the Wanapum Basalt. This flow, less than 14 my old,
        is one of the most widespread and easily recognized
        lavas of the Columbia River Group, since it always con-
        tains large crystals of feldspar (plagioclase phenocrysts).
        It came from a line of fissures 200 miles east of here,
        which spread their lavas over at least 15,000 square
        miles (with a volume of over 200 cubic miles!). It can
        best be examined by stopping a quarter mile ahead and
        walking back. (0.3)

13.1   Optional Stop. Chamberlain Lake Rest Area. Views
        west from here of Memaloose Island, formerly an Indian
        burial ground, and of a prominent lava flow which forms
        the skyline above the island. This flow is the *Pomona
        Member,* one of the last flows to come down the ances-
        tral Columbia River from Idaho about 12 my ago. It
        is the only Saddle Mountain flow in the Gorge, and
        has not been found west of Mosier, but there is some
        evidence that it may have gone clear to the ocean. It
        had about half the volume of the Roza Member. (1.0)

14.1   Roadcuts expose the base of the Pomona lava flow,
        which has a peculiar curved, pinch and swell columnar
        jointing resembling blades and splinters or spear-shaped
        slabs. (0.4)

14.5   Crossing axis of Mosier syncline. At 10:00 across the
        river to the southwest, the basin shape of the syncline
        can be seen in the down-fold of the Pomona Member.
        (1.7)

16.2   Junction with the west end of the Balch Lake road.
        Continue ahead. (0.6)

16.8   STOP. From here westward for several hundred feet,
        road cuts expose a sedimentary interbed between Wana-

pum Basalt flows that reveals a story of lava advancing into a lake and being shattered by the shock of exploding steam into a cross-bedded basaltic sandstone, composed of black glass grains and fragments of pillow lava. The next flow above the sandstone is a pillow lava, indicating that the lake was of some depth. (0.1)

16.9   Rounding Straits Point. The massive cliff above is the lowest Wanapum flow; from here on to Hood River, the Columbia River Basalt belongs to the Grande Ronde Member of the Yakima Basalt. The alcove and steep cliffs above Locke Lake on the right must have been formed by a great landslide, and since there is no debris at river level, the slide must have occurred before the Bretz flood, or at least 13,000 years ago. (1.2)

18.1   Exposures of the uppermost Grande Ronde Basalt flow. For the next 4 miles (to 21.8), the flows are numbered in paint on the rock faces from 1 to 11, as we enter the next fold to the west, the Bingen anticline. (1.3)

19.4   On the right a normal fault cuts Grande Ronde Basalt flow number 6. (0.4)

Looking across the Mosier syncline. Cliffs above the river are in three flows of Yakima Basalt which dip to the left (east); cliff in the distance beyond Mosier dips to the right (northwest). High bench and skyline are underlain by The Dalles Formation. (Sam Sargent photo)

19.8   Entering the town of Bingen, on the axis of the Bingen anticline. The fold can be seen across the river in the face of Burdoin Mountain (0.6)

20.4   Intersection with Highway 141, which goes north (right) to White Salmon. This town lies on a gravel bench 700 feet above the river. Immediately west of the town, is Little White Salmon volcano. This town may be the only one in Washington that lies on the flank of a shield volcano! (0.5)

20.9   Large quarries across the river are in basalt broken and sheared by the north-south trending Hood River fault, which crosses the river just east of the Hood River Bridge. White Salmon volcano may have come up along this fracture, which extends for many miles to the south. The Hood River Valley to the west of the fault has been dropped down (or the east side raised up) at least 2000 feet. The cliffs above in the thin lava flows of the volcano, were probably formed by erosion of the Bretz flood. A prominent mass of radiating fractures in the cliff represents the "war bonnet" structure which has been interpreted as the filling of a lava tube. They can also be seen in Broughton Bluff, just across the Sandy River from Troutdale. (0.9)

21.8   Junction with Hood River toll bridge. Continue west on highway 14. Huge boulders of White Salmon shield volcano olivine basalt have fallen down from the cliffs above and line the highway. Gravels similar to the Troutdale formation lie behind this talus, dropped down to river level by the Hood River fault. (0.2)

22.0   Junction with road leading to White Salmon. A good cross section of the lava flows from the volcano can be seen on this side road. At 12:00 on the skyline is another shield volcano, Underwood Mountain, capped by three small cinder cones. (1.2)

23.2   Optional stop. Exposures of palagonite tuff, breccia, and overlying pillow lava from White Salmon volcano indicates that these flows dammed the river, and the lava came out into a lake. (0.2)

23.4   Junction with White Salmon River road, leading north to Trout Lake and the Mount Adams country. (0.1)

23.5   Cross bridge over White Salmon River. Junction with
        road to Underwood Mountain and Cook. Excellent
        views on this side road of Mount Hood, Hood River
        Valley and the Gorge. This route is another good side
        trip, connecting with Highway 14 again at mile 30.8.
        (0.3)

23.8   STOP. Parking on left side of highway. Bluff exposes
        the Troutdale Formation, here consisting of the familiar
        quartzite-bearing conglomerate. Above the gravel is
        flood debris consisting of gravels with palagonite
        boulders and all is capped by basalt flows from Under-
        wood volcano. The flood material is from one of the
        earlier Spokane floods, certainly not the last Bretz flood.
        On a clear day, Mount Hood can be seen at 9:00 and
        Mount Defiance, a High Cascade shield volcano, at
        11:00. (0.5)

24.3   A block of tuff breccia from Underwood volcano is en-
        closed within Spokane flood deposits on the right. (0.2)

24.5   Fish hatchery on left. Cross Burlington Northern
        railroad tracks on the overpass and pass Broughton
        Lumber Mill on the right. This mill is the terminus
        of the last lumber flume operating in the United States.
        For the next 3 miles it can be seen crossing the bluffs
        above on its 9 mile course to the logging area on the
        Little White Salmon River. The flume frequently
        breaks during floods and freezes, and causes debris flows
        down the hill and across the highway. At 9:00 on the
        Oregon side, is Ruthton Point, noted for the fine display
        of brilliant yellow palagonite breccia, capped with High
        Cascade lavas. It is believed that this sub-aqueous flow
        came into a lake at a level of 400 feet, marking one
        of the major damming episodes on the Columbia River.
        (1.4)

25.9   Optional stop, at rest area on the left. Flat-lying Grande
        Ronde Basalt flows, exposed on the right, form the
        trough of the Underwood syncline. Southwest of here,
        it can be seen that the dips are to the southeast. (0.8)

26.7   Enter Tunnel no. 5 in Grande Ronde Basalt. Mitchell
        Point at 11:00. (0.7)

27.6   Cross railroad overpass. (0.2)

27.8   Drinking water available at right. (0.3)

28.1   Tunnel no. 3. Each of these tunnels are in the more
         resistant parts of Grande Ronde flows, which have been
         eroded out in ridges by the river and floods. (0.4)

28.5   Tunnel no. 2. (0.5)

29.0   Tunnel no. 1. Optional stop at west portal to tunnel,
         park on the left side of highway. The railroad and high-
         way cuts here exposes the top and bottom of a single,
         complete southeast-dipping flow of Grande Ronde
         Basalt. The upper part (entablature) is finely jointed
         (brickbat) basalt, the lower part (colonnade) is well de-
         veloped columnar-jointed basalt. In the cliffs above
         Drano Lake to the north may be seen a classical angular
         unconformity between the dipping basalts below and
         the horizontal Underwood Mountain lavas above. To
         the west lies the great uplifted mass of Cook Hill and
         Augspurger Mountain, the westernmost anticlinal fold
         in basalt exposed on the north side of the Gorge. A large
         northwest-trending fault passes beneath Drano Lake
         and over the east spur of Cook Hill, dropping it down
         on the northeast side. From here west, the folds trend
         northwest instead of northeast. (1.2)

30.2   Cross bridge over the Little White Salmon River to op-
         tional stop at road to right leading to fish hatchery.
         Up this road 500 feet is a well-exposed sedimentary in-
         terbed of sandstone lying between Grande Ronde lava
         flows. (0.2)

30.4   Crossing the axis of the small Cook Hill anticline, which
         plunges down to the southeast. Across the river to the
         south, it is apparent that the fold dies out rapidly. (0.4)

30.8   Junction with road leading to the towns of Cook, Under-
         wood, Willard, and the upper Little White Salmon
         River country. Side trip (from mile 23.5) rejoins the
         highway here. Note Mount Defiance volcano on the sky-
         line across the river at 10:00, and Dog Mountain at
         12:00. (0.6)

31.4   Note slickensided fault faces just west of Dog Creek
         crossing. This small fault parallels the axis of the Dog
         Mountain anticline. (2.0)

33.4   The Cascade or Pacific Crest Trail starts up Dog Mountain at this point. In the future, the trail will be routed west to cross the river at the Bridge of the Gods. Note the southwest dipping eroded hogbacks of Grande Ronde Basalt flows on the west flank of the Dog Mountain anticline. (0.6)

34.0   Passing Grant Lake on right. Note profile of Wind Mountain intrusive at 12:00 and the companion Shellrock Mountain intrusive (which does not reach the skyline) across the river at 9:30. You are crossing the Shellrock Mountain fault, which lies at the east contact of the intrusive across the river, and continues north to form the straight western escarpment of Dog Mountain. The west side of the fault has moved up at least 500 feet, exposing to erosion the soft Eagle Creek Formation beneath the Grande Ronde Basalt. (0.2)

34.2   Entering the Collins Point landslide, presently the most rapidly moving slide in the Gorge. Note the fresh but buckled and crooked macadam. This slide, beginning in the cliffs three miles to the north, covers 3 square miles, and the upper part moves as much as 45 feet per year. A Bonneville power line originally crossed the upper surface, but after numerous repairs and realignments, it had to be relocated high across the mountain to the north. (0.7)

34.9   Bergen Road junction on the right. A side trip up this road to the Girl Scout Camp displays recent displacement of the terrain, both horizontal and vertical. Fresh talus slopes and leaning trees on the right attest to the movements which produced the half mile bulge in the river bank below. (0.6)

35.5   Optional stop at abandoned quarry on the right to examine the Wind Mountain intrusive rock, which is a fine-grained hornblende-pyroxene quartz diorite. (0.5)

36.0   Note the broad smooth joint surfaces along the road cuts, quite different form any jointing seen elsewhere. Shellrock Mountain across the river is the southernmost of four large intrusions; Wind Mountain is the second one. Another lies above the head of the Collins Point landslide, yet another at King Mountain farther north. All intrude Grande Ronde Basalt, and hence are late Miocene or younger. (0.5)

36.5   West margin of Wind Mountain intrusion. The great
         west-dipping ridge on the skyline ahead is Stevenson
         Ridge, composed of lava flows of Three Corner Rock
         (Ohanepecosh Formation). Far ahead to the west are
         the summits of Table Mountain and Greenleaf Peak,
         capped by isolated remnants of Grande Ronde Basalt,
         filling ancient valleys eroded in the underlying Eagle
         Creek formation. Across the river, thin flows of Cascade
         lava cap the cliffs beneath Benson Plateau and Nick
         Eaton Ridge. (0.5)

37.0   Junction with Wind Mountain road. A large quarry half
         a mile up this road is in thick gravels lying upon older
         landslide material. The bluff ahead at 400 feet elevation
         across Wind River is the intracanyon lava flow which
         came 15 miles down Trout Creek from Trout Creek vol-
         cano, and dammed the Columbia River to produce the
         lake in which the delta gravels were deposited. (1.1)

38.1   Cross bridge over Wind River. (0.1)

38.2   Optional stop on right at junction with Hot Springs
         Road. An interesting 3-mile trip can be taken by follow-
         ing this road past St. Martins Hot Springs to Carson,
         rejoining the highway at mile 40.1. Road cuts en route
         up the hill expose a complex stratigraphy, with at least
         two sets of olivine basalt flows interbedded with lake
         beds, delta gravels from Wind River, volcanic ash, basal-
         tic sands, all topped by silt deposited in the Wind River
         embayment by the Bretz flood. The lake produced by
         these flows which dammed the Columbia River, possibly
         several times, must have been at least 350 feet deep.
         Here at the road junction, the gravels were probably
         deposited by an early Spokane flood. Good view from
         here of the landslide west of Wind Mountain, and across
         the river to Shellrock Mountain and Mount Defiance
         on the skyline. The straight northwest course of Wind
         River indicates that it followed a fault zone, with the
         southwest side dropped down. Evidence of the southeast
         continuation of this fault across the river can be seen
         in the notch in the north spur of Nick Eaton Ridge.
         For the next 2 miles, the rim above at 380 feet elevation
         lies above boulder talus from the uppermost intracan-
         yon flow. (1.3)

39.5   For the next 3 miles, roadcuts expose the oldest rocks

found at river level in the Gorge. This is the Ohanapecosh Formation, consisting of basalt flows and breccias.
Numerous small landslides have obscured the outcrops.
(0.6)

40.1   Junction with the Wind River road leading to Carson.
        Continue ahead, crossing more than half a mile of land-
        slide debris. (0.7)

40.8   Good exposures begin here, of Ohanapecosh lava flows,
        mudflow deposits, and volcaniclastic rocks, all slightly
        altered and metamorphosed with development of green-
        ish (zeolite) minerals. These have recently been separat-
        ed from the Ohanapecosh and called Lavas of Three
        Corner Rock. (0.7)

41.5   Benson Plateau lies on the skyline at 9:00 across the
        river, bordered by Herman Creek on the east. At river
        level opposite the mouth of Herman Creek are the intru-
        sive bodies of Government Cove Island and Sawmill.
        (1.5)

43.0   East city limits Stevenson, which is located upon the
        Eagle Creek Formation. (0.7)

43.7   Cross bridge over Rock Creek. From 12:00 to 2:00 is
        a fine view of the great Cascade landslide, which came
        down from Table Mountain and Greenleaf Peak on the
        skyline. The Red Bluffs beneath Greenleaf Peak are of
        bedded Eagle Creek Formation, and both peaks are
        capped by Grande Ronde Basalt. The Rabbit Ears, to
        the south (left) of Table Mountain are basalt dikes
        which intrude the Eagle Creek. Aldrich Butte, near the
        Columbia River, is a large block of Eagle Creek Forma-
        tion. The total landslide area covers nearly 14 square
        miles, but is composed of at least five tongues of land-
        slide material which came down at different times. The
        last one occurred about 1260 A.D., and shoved the chan-
        nel of the river more than a mile to the south, forming
        the Cascades of the Columbia. High Cascade lava from
        a nearly intact cinder cone located on the top of the
        cliff between Table Mountain and Greenleaf Peak over-
        lies on early slide, and is buckled and fissured by later
        sliding. Recent studies by the Corps of Engineers still
        fail to explain how such large blocks of lava (up to 200
        feet in size) could be moved intact (1.3)

45.0   Ashes Lake on the right is a remnant of the pre-land-
         slide main channel of the Columbia River. (0.4)

45.4   Entering the east margin of the Cascade landslide. Note
         the small lakes upon the hummocky surface. (0.4)

45.8   Junction with the Ashes Lake road; a side trip up this
         road gives one a spectacular view of the chaotic nature
         of a large slide. (0.2)

46.0   Junction with Bridge of the Gods. Here, one has the
         option of a quick return to Portland via the south side
         freeway. It is quite probable that the Indians' legend
         of the Bridge of the Gods resulted from their use of
         the landslide dam, before it was washed out. (0.5)

46.5   The lava rim of Sheridan Point on the right is a huge
         mass of lava brought down intact from above. (0.6)

47.1   Cross railroad overpass. The railroad tunnel in the land-
         slide lies on the right. Eagle and Tanner Creeks, from
         8:00 to 10:00, are major side canyons cut deeply into
         the south wall of the Gorge, with Wauna Point between.
         The bare ridge of Munra Point lies west of Tanner
         Creek. (0.6)

47.7   The new powerhouse for Bonneville Dam lies on the
         old town site of North Bonneville. Slide material was
         removed down to a bedrock knob of solid Eagle Creek
         Formation which once formed part of the south bank
         of the Columbia River. The new highway follows the
         approximate former course of the river. At 9:00 is Bon-
         neville Dam, whose south abutment is anchored in Bon-
         ney Rock, a 250 foot wide dike of basalt similar to that
         of the Rabbit Ears. (1.2)

48.9   Junction with road to right leading to Moffets Hot
         Springs. This is the western edge of the Cascade Range
         hot springs zone, which extends south for over a

Historical view (about 1920) of Table Mountain with Aldrich Butte in the foreground, showing the effects of the
Yacolt fires of 1902 and 1910. Table Mountain is capped
by Yakima Basalt, lying above Eagle Creek Formation,
which is best exposed in the light-colored cliffs of Greenleaf
Peak, above the Cascade Landslide in the upper right. Note
the fishwheel on the right (Historical Society photo).

hundred miles through Austin Hot Springs on the
Clackamas River, Breitenbush Hot Springs on the San-
tiam, Belknap and Foley Hot Springs on the McKenzie
River, and McCreadie and Kitson Hot Springs on the
Willamette River. On the Columbia River, the zone is
about 10 miles wide and contains 5 springs. (1.1)

50.0   New town of Bonneville on the left. Aldrich Butte lies
        above at 3:00. (0.1)

50.1   Bridge over Hamilton Creek. Hamilton Mountain to the
        north is a fine example of "reversed topography". It is
        mostly composed of horizontally bedded Eagle Creek
        Formation, in which an ancient valley was cut, and then
        filled with an intracanyon flow of Grande Ronde Basalt,
        which extends only about 2 miles to the north of the
        summit. The softer Eagle Creek sediments have been
        eroded away, leaving the lava-filled valley high on the
        north wall of the Gorge. The west side of the valley
        includes foreset-bedded palagonite tuff deposited in a
        lake caused by the damming of this ancient stream. The
        spectacular pinnacle of Beacon Rock looms ahead at
        12:00. (1.8)

51.9   Cross Hardy Creek. View south to Nesmith Point, a
        half-eroded High Cascade Basalt volcano on the rim,
        with Yeon Mountain to the west, rimmed by lava flows
        from the same volcano, and St. Peters Dome, an isolated
        peak of Grande Ronde Basalt flows set out from the
        Gorge wall below the rim. (1.1)

53.0   STOP. Beacon Rock State Park, with rest rooms and
        fountain. Park on the left. A picnic area lies up the
        hill to the north. Beacon Rock, named by Lewis and
        Clark in 1806, is a volcanic plug or neck of olivine basalt.
        It is *not* a "monolith", since it is broken by differently
        oriented columnar joints and has irregular fluidal layer-
        ing within the mass, typical of the filling of the throat
        of a volcano which has now been largely eroded away.
        The mass of olivine basalt a mile to the north above
        the upper picnic area is probably also a part of this
        volcano. A trail and stairway with 48 switchbacks was
        laboriously constructed by the original owner who do-
        nated it to the state. It climbs the 500 feet to the sum-
        mit at 840 feet above the river, and affords a splendid
        view up and down the river. For the next 10 miles to

Cape Horn viewpoint, road cuts are in landslide material, mostly of the Eagle Creek Formation. Boulders in the cuts are mostly of pyroxene andesite. (0.8)

53.8   Cross Woodward Creek. Road to the left leads to a lower campground and boat moorage. (1.2)

55.0   Passing through town of Skamania, an Indian name meaning "swift waters". (1.3)

56.3   Franz Road junction on right. Huge landslide blocks to be seen alongside the highway are of Grande Ronde Basalt, from Archer Mountain and the long narrow Prindle Mountain on the skyline ahead. Views of the Gorge waterfalls may be seen across the river. (5.4)

61.7   Junction with Highway 140, leading north to the Washougal River. For the next two miles we will pass around the head of the Cape Horn landslide. The cliffs of Cape Horn are of Grande Ronde Basalt, overlain by Troutdale Formation and by High Cascade (Boring) lavas to form an upland surface. Note the long ridge of basalt below to the left, which has dropped down and pulled away from the upper slopes to form a landslide valley. (1.3)

63.0   Highway cut exposes three flows of Grande Ronde Basalt. Steel netting is necessary to prevent rocks from falling on the highway. Several pull-offs on left provide excellent views of the Gorge, but continue ahead to main stop. (0.3)

63.3   STOP. Cape Horn viewpoint. Park on the left. Looking east to Beacon Rock at 12:00, you can see Bobs Mountain at 10:00, one of a north-south line of High Cascade (Boring) cinder cones, so recent that parts of their crater depressions are still preserved. At 11:00 other cinder cones cap the ridge to the north of Prindle Mountain, which, like Archer Mountain in the middle distance and Hamilton Mountain beyond are all composed of Grande Ronde Basalt. The subdued topography beneath the cliffs are landslides. At 2:00 Phoca Rock (named after the harbor seal, *Phoca vitulina,* which inhabited the river in early days) is a remnant of the Cape Horn landslide, which probably post-dates the Bretz flood. On the skyline above Phoca Rock is Larch Mountain, the highest (over 4000 feet elevation) and largest shield volcano of High Cascade Basalt near the west part of the Gorge. The cliffs beneath are crested by Angels Rest and Devils Rest. Palmer Peak and Nesmith Point volcanos are seen farther up the river at 1:00. Pepper Mountain, can be seen at 3:00. The roadcut across the highway exposes loessal soil resting on bouldery gravels of flood origin on top of Grande Ronde Basalt. At least 3 flows of basalt occur above and 2 below the highway. Here the total thickness of flows are less than 800 feet near the river, and they thin to 200 feet within 2 miles to the north, suggesting that they lapped against the north wall of the Miocene canyon. During the next mile west, we will cross outcrops of Boring lava from Mount Zion volcano, which lies less than a mile northwest of here. (0.9)

64.2   The highway crosses the surface of the Boring lavas. Crown Point lies at 11:00 across the river. (0.5)

64.7   Roadcut exposes a narrow vertical fissure zone of volcanic scoria, breccia and slabby jointed olivine basalt, possible a minor vent on the south slope of Mount Zion volcano. Directly below this point the south-dipping upper surface of the Grande Ronde Basalt plunges below river level. This is almost 4 miles east of the point where it goes below river level on the south side at Corbett Station, suggesting that there may be a fault beneath the river, with the south side either dropped down, moved to the west, or both. (0.1)

64.8   Junction with Belle Center road. Outcrops are of olivine basalt from Mount Pleasant, another Boring lava cinder cone which lies one mile to the northwest. (0.4)

65.2   Marble Road junction. (0.2)

65.4   Bretz flood gravels, deposited at 700 feet elevation, here overlie Troutdale Formation conglomerates. (0.7)

66.1   STOP. Park on left. Good exposures of Troutdale Formation, the ancient river deposits that filled the ancestral valley and basins during Pliocene time. The varied composition of the cobbles and pebbles tells us much about the geologic history of the river. Although many of the pebbles are of volcanic rocks abundant in the Cascade Range, both plutonic and metamorphic rocks also occur, rocks that must have come more than 300 miles from the upper reaches of the river in British Columbia and the Rocky Mountains. The light-colored pebbles of quartzite (a metamorphosed sandstone) are especially characteristic of the Troutdale Formation. Note also the shingle-like arrangement of the cobbles, and the west-dipping foreset bedding, which indicate that the river also flowed from east to west more than 2 million years ago. Numerous outcrops of Troutdale Formation for the next mile. (1.0)

67.1 Cross Lawton Creek. Numerous large boulders of olivine basalt were probably derived from the Mount Pleasant lava flows, undermined by the Bretz floodwaters and rolled down the hill. Chamberlain Hill, another Boring volcano, lies across the river at 10:00, capping slopes of Troutdale at Broughton Bluff, east of the town of Troutdale. (1.8)

68.9 Exit to Evergreen Boulevard; continue on main highway. You are now crossing the modern floodplain of the Columbia River, with east Portland in view on the left. Prune Hill, composed of Troutdale Formation, lies at 12:00 above the town of Camas. It is capped on the south and west spurs by two small cinder cones, the westernmost volcanos to be seen on the Washington side of the river. A thick lava flow from one of these vents has been mined for many years in the Fisher Quarries for jetty rock. (2.8)

71.7 Junction with highway 140 to Washougal and the Washougal River country. At 4:00 on the skyline, Silver Star Mountain rises to 4650 feet elevation. It is composed of Ohanapecosh Formation, intruded on the east slopes by the Silver Star stock, a deep-seated intrusion of granodiorite and quartzdiorite, whose hot juices formed a few small copper deposits. This stock is the nearest granitic intrusion to Portland. The low-lying hills immediately north of Washougal are also Ohanapecosh Formation (locally known as Skamania Volcanics), surrounded and overlapped by Troutdale Formation. In the Miocene they were hills lying north of the main Columbia River valley, and high enough never to have been covered by any of the floods of Yakima Basalt. (1.5)

73.2   Junction with highway 500 leading to the town of Camas at 2:00, identified both visually and olifactorially by the paper mills. (1.2)

74.4   Cross Camas Slough. Prune Hill, above the paper mill, like the hills in east Portland, is composed largely of Troutdale Formation, which has been cemented by mineral waters heated by an intrusion of Boring basalt, so that it (and Mount Tabor, Kelly Butte and others) became resistant to erosion by the Bretz floodwaters. (0.3)

74.7   Settling ponds on the left are for disposal of wastewater from the paper mills. (0.4)

75.1   Cross bridge across lower Camas Slough. The south-dipping layers exposed north of the slough are part of the Ohanapecosh Formation, overlain by Troutdale Formation. (0.4)

75.5   TAKE EXIT on right to Northwest 6th Avenue. (0.3)

75.8   At stop sign, turn right onto 6th Avenue, and prepare to turn right again. (0.3)

76.1   Turn right (south) onto Northwest 7th Avenue. (0.2)

76.3   STOP. Park on right. The roadcut on the left (southeast) exposes three units within the south-dipping Ohanapecosh Formation. Just above the road are beds of tuff (consolidated volcanic ash), overlain by basaltic flow-breccia, and capped by a blocky-jointed porphyritic basalt lava flow. To continue westward, drive ahead, but before crossing overpass make a U-turn and return to Northwest 6th Avenue. (0.4)

76.7   Stop sign. Turn left (west) onto Northwest 6th Avenue. (0.7)

77.4   Merge on left with highway 14 to Vancouver. (0.7)

78.1   Blocky jointed flows of Boring Lava from Prune Hill volcano overlie nearly flatlying tuff beds of the Ohanapecosh Formation. (0.4)

78.5   Roadcut on right exposes southwest-dipping altered basaltic breccia of the Ohanapecosh Formation. (0.8)

79.3   Brady Road on the right climbs the flank of Prune Hill
        volcano, which caps the west part of main Prune Hill.
        (0.3)

79.6   Roadcuts on right expose Boring Lava. (0.5)

80.1   Fisher Quarry on the right. Boring lava from Prune Hill
        volcano has been mined for many years to supply giant
        blocks for the jetties at the mouth of the Columbia.
        They are trucked beneath the highway overpass to the
        loading facilities at 3:00, and barged down river. (0.2)

80.3   The last outcrop of Boring lava appears on the left.
        The masonry yard on the right is where the blocks are
        trimmed and shaped when used for construction pur-
        poses. (0.5)

80.8   Continue past exit to Southeast 164th Avenue on right.
        (1.5)

82.3   Enter area of new housing developments, the fastest
        growing city in Washington. The great boulders scat-
        tered around were torn from the Prune Hill lava flow
        and carried here by the Bretz flood. (0.7)

83.0   Exit to Interstate Highway 205 and to the new Inter-
        state bridge. For those going north this is the quickest
        route, and when the bridge is completed, it will be the
        quickest route south as well. The next 7 miles to Van-
        couver and the Interstate 5 bridge continues west on
        the delta deposits of the Spokane and Bretz floods which
        mantle the plains on both sides of the river.

PART III
APPENDICES

BIBLIOGRAPHY

"Researchers have already cast much darkness on the subject, and if they continue their investigations, we shall soon know nothing at all about it."

Mark Twain

It is the fond hope of the author, who has been a field geologist for over 15 years and a geology teacher for nearly 30 years, that the reader may have become sufficiently interested in the subject to pursue it a little further!

This is the reason I have included references to sources scattered throughout the text. In addition, there are several fine sources of information on the geology of the entire Northwest which may be of value to those who travel beyond the confines of the Gorge. The following five annotated references can be obtained from libraries, book stores or from the Oregon Department of Geology and Mineral Industries:

McKee (1972): Nearly 400 pages of non-technical geologic history of Oregon, Washington, Idaho and British Columbia. Amply illustrated, and contains over 30 trip guides.

Corcoran (1969): The best brief summary of the geology of Oregon, and a more detailed survey of its mineral and water resources, with maps showing the location of more than 50 mineral and rock commodities.

Baldwin (1976): A longer and more technical review of the geology of Oregon, used for many years as a university text on the subject.

Beaulieu (1973): Brief summaries and detailed road logs for seven field trips in central and northern Oregon and southern Washington.

Wells and Peck (1961) and Walker (1977): Large detailed geologic maps of western and eastern Oregon.

Allen, J.E., 1933, Contributions to the structure, stratigraphy and petrography of the lower Columbia River Gorge, M.A. thesis, Univ. of Oregon, 96 p.

____, 1958, Columbia River Gorge, Portland to The Dalles (In) Guidebook for Field Trip Excursions, Cord. Sec., Geol. Soc. America, Univ. of Oregon, p. 4-23.

Allison, I.S., 1935, Glacial erratics in the Willamette Valley, Geol. Soc. America Bull., v. 46, 605-632.

Baker, V.R., 1973, Paleohydrology and sedimentology of Lake Missoula flooding in eastern Washington, Geol. Soc. America, Spec. Paper 144, 79 pp.

____ and Nummedal, Dag, 1978, The channeled scabland, a guide to the geomorphology of the Columbia Basin, Washington, Planetary Geology Program, Office of Space Science, Nat. Aeronautics and Space Adm., Wash., D.C. 186 p.

Baldwin, E.M., 1976, Geology of Oregon (rev. ed.), Kendall-Hunt, 147 p.

Balsillie, J.H. and G.T. Benson, 1971, Evidence for the Portland Hills fault, Ore. Dept. Geology and Mineral Industries, Ore Bin, v. 33, p. 109-118.

Beaulieu, J.D., Ed., 1973, Geologic field trips in northern Oregon and southern Washington, Ore. Dept. Geology and Mineral Industries, Bull. 77, 206 p.

Beeson, M.H., Moran, M.R. and Olson, F.L., 1976, Geochemical data on Columbia River Basalt stratigraphy in western Oregon, Geol. Soc. America, Abs. with Programs, v. 8, p. 354.

____ and Nelson, D.O., 1978, A model for development of Mount Tabor, Kelly Butte, and Powell Butte in southeast Portland, Ore. Acad. Sci., 36th Ann. Mtg., Linfield College, McMinnville, Ore., Feb. 27.

____ and Moran, M.R., 1979, Columbia River Basalt Group stratigraphy in western Oregon, Oregon Geology, v. 41, n. 1, Jan., p. 11-14.

____ and Perttu, R. and J., 1978, The origin of Miocene basalts of coastal Oregon and Washington — an alternate hypothesis, unpublished mss.

Bretz, J.H., Smith, H.T.U. and Neff, G.E., 1956, Channeled scabland of Washington, new data and interpretations, Geol. Soc. America Bull., v. 67, p. 957-1049.

Bretz, J.H., 1969, The Lake Missoula floods and the channeled scablands, Jour. Geology, v. 77, p. 503-43.

Chaney, R.W., 1920, The flora of the Eagle Creek Formation (Washington and Oregon), Univ. Chicago, Walker Museum Contr., v. 2, no. 5, p. 115-181.

____, 1948, The ancient forests of Oregon, Oregon Univ. Press, 56 p.

Corcoran, R.E., 1969, General geologic history of Oregon (In) Mineral and water resources of Oregon, Ore. Dept. Geology and Min. Res., Bull. 64, p. 23-32.

Felts, W.M., 1939, A granodiorite stock in the Cascade Mountains of southwestern Washington, Ohio Jour. Sci., v. 39, p. 297-316.

Free, M.R., 1976, Evidence for magmatic assimilation in several diorites of the middle Columbia River Gorge (M.S. thesis), Univ. Utah, Salt Lake City, Utah, 65 p.

Gary, M., McAfee, R. Jr., Wolf, C.L., (editors), 1972, Glossary of geology, American Geol. Inst., 805 p.

Grant, A.R., 1969, Chemical and physical controls for base metal deposition in the Cascade Range of Washington, Wash. Div. Mines and Geol., Bull. no. 58, 107 p.

Hammond, Paul E., 1979, Reconnaissance geologic map and cross-sections of southern Washington Cascade Range, Department of Earth Sciences, Portland State University, 2 sheets, 48x60 inches, color, 20 p.

Harris, S.L., 1976, Fire and ice — the Cascade volcanoes, The Mountaineers-Pacific Search Books, 320 p.

Hodge, E.T., 1938, Geology of the lower Columbia River, Geol. Soc. Amer. Bull., v. 49, no. 6, p. 831-930.

Johnson, A.G., 1977, Microearthquakes near Portland, Oregon (abs.), EOS, v. 58, no. 3, p. 168.

Lawrence, D.B. and E.G., 1958, Bridge of the Gods Legend, its origin, history, and dating, Mazama, v. 40, no. 13, p. 33-41.

Lentz, Rodney Thomas, (1977), The petrology and stratigraphy of the Portland Hills Silt, Portland State University, M.S. Thesis, 144 p.

Mackin, J.H., and Carey, A.S., 1965, Origin of Cascade landscapes, Wash. Div. of Mines and Geology, Inform. Circ. no. 41, 35 p.

McKee, Bates, 1972, Cascadia, the geologic evolution of the Pacific Northwest, McGraw-Hill, 394 p.

Newcomb, R.C., 1969, Effect of tectonic structure on the occurrence of ground water in the basalt of the Columbia River Group of The Dalles area, Oregon and Washington, U.S. Geol. Survey Prof. Paper 383-C, 33 p.

Newton, V.C., Jr., 1969, Subsurface geology of the lower Columbia and Willamette basins, Ore. Dept. Geol. and Min. Ind., Oil and Gas Inves. no. 2, 121 p.

Palmer, L., 1977, Large landslides of the Columbia River Gorge, Oregon and Washington, p. 69-83 in Choates, D.C., ed., Landslides: Geol. Soc. Amer. Reviews in Engineering Geology, v. III, p. 69-83.

Schaffer, J., Hartline, B. and Hartline, F., 1974, The Pacific Crest Trail, Volume 2: Oregon and Washington, Wilderness Press, 346 p.

Snavely, P.D., Jr., Macleod, N.S. and Wagner, H.C., 1973, Miocene tholeiitic basalts of coastal Oregon and Washington and their coeval basalts of the Columbia Plateau, Geol. Soc. Amer. Bull., v. 84, no. 2, p. 387-424.

Snavely, P.D., Jr., and Wagner, H.C., 1963, Tertiary geologic history of western Oregon and Washington, Washington Div. of Mines and Geology, Dept. of Inv. No. 22, 25 p.

Strong, Emory, 1959, Stone age on the Columbia River, Binfords and Mort, 254 p.

Treasher, R.C., 1942, Geologic history of the Portland (Oregon) area, Oregon Dept. of Geology and Min. Industries, Short Paper 7, 17 p.

Trimble, D.E., 1963, Geology of Portland, Oregon, and adjacent areas, U.S. Geol. Survey Bull. 1119, 119 p.

Waters, A.C., 1960, Determining direction of flow in basalts, Amer. Jour. Sci., v. 258-A (Bradley Vol.), p. 350-366.

_____, 1961, Stratigraphic and lithologic variations in the Columbia River Basalt, American Jour. of Science, v. 259, p. 583-611.

_____, 1973, The Columbia River Gorge: Basalt stratigraphy, ancient lava dams and landslide dams, p. 133-162, in Beaulieu, J.D., Geologic field trips in northern Oregon and southern Washington, Ore. Dept. Geol. and Min. Ind., Bull. 77, 206 p.

Weis, Paul L., and Newman, William L., 1973, The channeled scabland of eastern Washington — the geologic story of the Spokane Flood, U.S. Geol. Survey pamphlet, 25 p. 23 figs.

Wells, F.D., and Peck, D., 1961, Geologic Map of Oregon west of the 120th meridian, U.S. Geol. Survey Misc. Inv. Map I-325.

Williams, I.A., 1916, The Columbia River Gorge, its geologic history interpreted from the Columbia River Highway, Ore. Bur. of Mines and Geology, Mineral Resources of Oregon, v. 2 no. 3, 130 p.

Wise, W.S., 1961, The geology and mineralogy of the Wind River area, Washington, and the stability relations of celadonite, Baltimore, Md., The Johns Hopkins Univ. (Ph.D. thesis), 258 p.

_____, 1970, Cenozoic volcanism in the Cascade Mountains of southern Washington, Wash. Div. Mines and Geol., Bull. no. 60, 45 p.

Woodburne, M.O. and Robinson, P.T., 1977, A new late Hemingford mammal fauna from the John Day Formation, Oregon, Journ. of Paleontology, v. 51, n. 4, p. 752.

Wright, T.L, Grolier, M.J. and Swanson, D.A., 1973, Chemical variation related to the stratigraphy of the Columbia River Basalt, Geol. Soc. Amer. Bull., v. 84, no. 2, p. 371-383.

INDEX AND GLOSSARY

Italicised words are technical terms whose definitions are given, usually at the first page referenced.
Italicised page numbers refers to figures, photographs and tables.

A

Aldrich Butte: 27, *94,* 125, *126,* 128
Andesite: 6, 7, 39, *42,* 70, 71, 92, 129
Angels Rest: 85, 89, 130
Anticlines: 13, 16, 40, 41, 115; (see also Bingen; 41, 103, *104,* 106; Cook Hill; 122; Dog Mountain, 102, 122; Ortley, 40, 41, 106, *108,* 109, 112, *113, 114,* 115, *116, 117;* Portland Hills, *13,* 16, 40, *75)*
Archer Mountain: 85, 92, *113,* 129
Ash (see also tuff): 6, 7, 15, 17, 18, 34, 36, 39, 43, 56, 57, 98, 124, 132
Ashes Lake: 127
Augspurger Mountain: *41,* 101, 122

B

Basalt: 6, 7, *11,* 18, 24, 36, 37, 39, *42,* 70, 71, 86, 101, 106, 124, 125, 128, 130, 131, 132 (see also Yakima Basalt, Boring and Cascade Lavas, etc.)
Basalt floods: 11, 18, 34, 35, *36, 37,* 38, 44, 57
Beacon Rock: 27, 28, 60, 70, 71, 84, 85, 92, *93, 113,* 128, 129
Benson Plateau: 10, 24, *25,* 92, 98, 124, 125
Bingen anticline: 41, 103, *104,* 106, 113, 120
Bobs Mountain: 129
Bonneville: 22, 28, 49, 52, *55,* 56, 60, 61, 62, 64, *93,* 96, 127, 128

Bonney Rock: 96, 127
Boring Lavas: 4, *13, 35,* 40, *43,* 57, 69, 73, *74, 75,* 81, 82, 84, 85, 86, *88,* 89, 129, 130, 131, 132, 133
Breccia: 6, 7, 15, 34, 69, 70, 101, 103, 116, 120, 121, 125, 130, 132
Bretz flood: *43,* 49, 50, 51, 52, 57, 60, 68, *80, 104, 105,* 106, *109,* 111, 112, *114,* 115, 116, 117, 118, 120, 121, 124, 129, 130, 131, 132, 133 (see also Missoula, Spokane, Glacial floods)
Bridal Veil: *26,* 87, 89, 102
Bridge of the Gods: xi, 19, *55,* 56, 60, 63, 64, 72, *95,* 98, 123, 127
Broughton Bluff: 82, 120, 131
Bull Run: 28

C

Camas: 71, 113, 131, 132
Camping facilities: 76-77
Cape Horn: 28, 52, 62, 64, 89, 129
Cascade landslide: *43,* 49, 52, *54, 55,* 56, 57, 60, *94, 95,* 96, *97,* 98, 125, *126,* 127
Cascade Lavas: 4, *11,* 18, 23, 24, *35,* 40, 57, 69, 70, 85, *88,* 89, 92, 96, 109, 121, 124, 125, 128, 129, 130
Cascade Locks: 56, 62, 63, 64, 71, 98
Cascades of the Columbia: ix, 23, *55,* 56, 60, 61, 62, 63, 64, 125
Cenozoic: 2, 32, 52

Chamberlain Hill: 4, *11, 13,* 82, 131

Chamberlain Lake: 118

Cinder cones: 5, 11, 18, 23, 24, 52, *53,* 69, 74, *75,* 120, 129, 131

Cirques: 10, 46, 92

Clarno Formation: 34, *35*

Coal: *33,* 34, 70

Collins Point landslide: see Wind Mountain landslide

Colonnade: 9, 89, *90,* 97, 102, 106, 122

Columbia River Basalt Group: 37 (see mostly Yakima Basalt, also Imnaha Basalt and Picture Gorge Basalt)

Columbia River: dams, ix, *22,* 64, 65, 111, *112;* statistics, 21, *22*

Columbia Triangle: 31, *32,* 33, 34, 38

Composite volcanos: 11, 18, 23, 24, 40, *42*

Conglomerate: 7, 39, 69, 70, 71, 81, 82, 86, 101

Cook Hill anticline: 122

Coopey Falls: *26*

Corbett: 84, 130

Council Crest: 72, 73, 79

Cretaceous: 2, 17, 32, 33

Cross-section: 12, *13, 78, 113*

Crown Point: 26, 28, 30, 50, 51, 70, *83,* 84, 85, 86, *87,* 130

D

Dalles Formation: see The Dalles Formation

Dacite: 6, 70

Dams: Bonneville, 64, 96; The Dalles, 65, 111, *112* (see also lava dams, landslide dams)

Deltas: 10, *33,* 34, 82, 124

Devils Rest: 85, 89, 130

Diabase: 6, 96

Dikes: 5, 10, *36, 37,* 38, *55,* 70, 92, 96, 118, 125, 127

Diktytaxitic: 98

Dog Mountain: 28, *48,* 52, 71, *95, 100,* 101, 102, *113,* 122, 123

Dog Mountain anticline: 102, 122

E

Eagle Creek: xi, 24, *25,* 26, 46, 70, 98, 127

Eagle Creek Formation: 4, 12, 27, *35,* 36, 52, *55,* 57, 68, 70, *78, 88,* 89, 92, *94,* 96, 98, 99, 101, *113,* 123, 124, 125, *126,* 127, 128, 129

Earthquakes: 16, 47, 49, 51, 52

Ellensberg Formation: 38

Elowah Falls: *26,* 96

Entablature: 9, 89, *90,* 102, 122

Eocene: xi, *2,* 3, 17, 33, *35*

Epoch: 2, 3

Era: 2, 3, 9

Escarpments: 10, *42,* 48, 49, 74, 103

Estacada Formation: 43, 47, 69

Extrusives: 5, 6 (see also Boring, Cascade Lavas, Yakima Basalt)

F

Faults: 8, 10, *13,* 16, 47, 78, 102, 103, 111, *113,* 122, 124, 130 (See also Hood River, *42, 48,* 49, 103, *113,* 120; Portland Hills, 13, *48,* 74; Rowena Gap, 116, Shellrock Mountain, 102, 123)

Fifes Peak Formation: *35,* 70

Fisher quarries: 131, 133

Five Mile Rapids: 59

Formations: 3, 4, 12, 68-71 (see also formational names: ie Yakima Basalt)

Fossils: xi, 10, 12, 18, 19, 34, 44, 89, 91, 97, 110

Fountain landslide: *54,* 56, 99

H

Glacial erratics: 50, 69

Glacial floods: 18, *43,* 46, 47, 49, 50, 51, 52, 57, 59, 60, 68, 74, *80, 104, 105,* 106, *107, 109,* 111, 112, *114,* 115, 116, 117, 118, 120, 121, 124, 129, 130, 131, 132, 133 (see also Bretz, Missoula and Spokane floods)

Glacial lakes: Allison, *45,* 51; Condon, *45,* 50; Lewis, *45,* 50; Missoula, *45,* 50

Glaciation: 19, 24, 29, 44, 46, 59, 103
Government Island: 98, 125
Grande Ronde Basalt: 35, 37, 38, *55,* 70, 115, 116, 119, 121, 122, 123, 124, 125, 128, 129, 130
Granodiorite: (see Quartz-diorite)
Greenleaf Peak: *55,* 70, *94,* 124, 125, *126*
Green Point Mountain: 40, 46
Gresham Formation: 43, 47, 69

H
Hamilton Mountain: 60, 70, 92, *113,* 128, 129
Hanging valleys: 10, 51
Hercules Pillars: 87
Herman Creek: 25, 70, 98, 99, 125
Highland Butte: 75
Holocene: 2, 4, 23, 24, *43,* 52, 68
Hood River: 4, 10, 16, 24, *25,* 28, 30, 40, *41,* 46, 50, 51, 52, *53,* 60, 70, 72, *78,* 103, 120, 121
Hood River anticline: (see Bingen anticline)
Hood River graben: *113*
Hood River fault: *42, 48,* 49, 103, *113,* 120
Hood River syncline: 103
Horsetail Falls: *26,* 92
Hot Springs: 124, 127, 128

I
Ice Age: (see Pleistocene)
Igneous rocks: 5, 6, 15
Imnaha Basalt: 37, 38
Incised meanders: 10, 47, 82
Intracanyon Lavas: 41, 43, 69, *95,* 99, 102, 103, *113,* 124, 128
Intrusives: 5, 6, 71, 101, 123, 124

J
John Day Formation: 34, *35,* 36

K
Kelly Butte: 51, 72, 73, *75,* 132
Klickitat River: 28, 72, 106, *113,* 117

L
Landslides: 19, 29, *43,* 52, *54, 55,* 56, 57, 60, 68, 74, 79, *83,* 84, 85, 91, *97,* 98, 99, *100,* 123, 124, *126,* 127, 129
Landslide dams: 52, *54, 55,* 56, 57, 60, 125
Larch Mountain: 4, *11,* 24, *25,* 39, *43,* 46, 72, *75, 78,* 81, 84, 85, 86, 101, 129
Lapilli: 6, 7
Latourelle Falls: *26,* 86
Laurel Hill: 38
Lava dams: 18, *41, 43,* 44, 57, 99, 102, 103, 121, 124, 128
Lavas of Three Corner Rock: 55, 70, 124, 125
Lewis and Clark: xi, 28, 60, 89, 91, 92, *93,* 128
Lindsey Creek: *26,* 102
Lithification: 15
Little Butte Series: 34
Little White Salmon River: 4, 28, *41,* 57, 102, *113,* 120, 121, 122
Loess: 19, 47, 73, 130
Long Narrows: 111, *112*
Lyle: 72, 106, *107,* 117

M
Magma: 5, 14, 15
Man in the Gorge: 59-65 (see also Prehistoric man)
Mantle: 14
Mayer State Park: 50, *105,* 106, 117
McCord Creek: *26,* 70, 96
Memaloose Island: 118
Mesa: 10, *105*
Mesozoic: 2, 32, 33
Metamorphic rocks: 5, *15,* 39, 70, 71, 125, 130
Miocene: 2, 4, 18, 24, 34, *35,* 36, 38, 39, 70, 96, 123, 130, 131
Missoula floods: 49, 57, 68 (see also Bretz, Spokane, Glacial floods)
Mist Falls: *26*
Mitchell Point: 27, 28, 102, 103, *104,* 121
Moffett Creek: *26,* 96

Mosier: 50, 69, 70, 72, *78*, 105, 106, 118

Mosier syncline: 40, 41, *104, 105,* 106, *113, 114,* 118, *119*

Mount Adams: 4, 23, *32,* 40, *42,* 46, 72, *94,* 103, *114,* 117, 120

Mount Defiance: 4, 24, *25,* 40, *41, 43,* 46, 57, *78,* 101, 121, 122, 124

Mount Hood: 4, *11,* 23, *32,* 38, 40, 46, 52, 60, 61, 72, *74,* 101, 103, 112, 121

Mount Pleasant: 4, 84, 85, *113,* 130, 131

Mount Scott: 51, 72, 73, *75*

Mount St. Helens: 4, *11,* 23, *32, 43,* 46, 52, 61, 72

Mount Sylvania: 73, *75*

Mount Tabor: *11, 13,* 51, 72, 73, *75, 78, 80,* 81, 132

Mount Talapus: 39, 46

Mount Zion: 4, *11,* 84, 85, 89, *113,* 130

Multnomah Falls: 26, 28, 64, 65, 70, 89, *90,* 91

Mudflows: 34, 36, 56, 57, 74, 125

Munra Point: 127

N

Nesmith Point: 92, 128, 130

Nick Eaton Ridge: 124

O

Ohanapecosh Formation: 4, 5, 34, *35,* 52, 57, 70, 71, *78, 94,* 101, *113,* 124, 125, 131, 132

Oligocene: 2, 4, 18, 34, *35,* 71

Oneonta Gorge: 26, 70, *88,* 91

Ortley anticline: 40, 41, 106, *108,* 109, 112, *113, 114,* 115, *116, 117*

P

Palagonite: 110, 103, 119, 120, 121, 128

Palmer Peak: 130

Palouse Formation: 47

Parkdale lava: *43, 53,* 60

Parks: 76-77

Pepper Mountain: 84, 85, 130

Perham Creek: 102

Period: 2, 3, 9

Permian: 2, 33

Phoca Rock: 84, 85, 129

Picture Gorge Basalt: 35, 37, 38

Pillow lavas: 86, 90, 103, *110,* 119, 120

Pinnacles: xii, *27,* 28, *87*

Plate tectonics: 14

Pleistocene: 2, 4, 23, 24, *43,* 44, 46, 47, 49, 50, 51, 69, 73, 101

Pliocene: 2, 4, 18, 23, *35,* 39, 40, 44, 49, 69, 71, 92, 101, 110, 130

Pomona Basalt Member: *107,* 118

Porphyry: 6, 118, 132

Portland Hills: 73, *75*

Portland Hills anticline: *13,* 16, 40, *75*

Portland Hills fault: *13, 48,* 73

Portland Hills Silt: 4, *13, 43,* 47, 69, 73, 79

Portland syncline: 4, *13,* 16, 40, 70, 73, *75*

Prehistoric man: 59, 60, 111, 127

Priest Rapids Basalt Member: *107*

Prindle Mountain: 129

Prune Hill: *113,* 131, 132, 133

Q

Quartz-diorite (including grano-diorite): ii, *6,* 7, 38, 71, 99, *100,* 101, 123, 131

Quartzite: 39, 70, 82, 89, 102, 103, 131

Quaternary: 2, 40, *41,* 46, 56, 68, 69

R

Rabbit Ears: 125, 127

Recent: (see Holocene)

Red Bluffs: 125

Rest stops: 76-77

Rhododendron Formation: 35, 39, *42,* 57, 70, 98

Rock Creek: 70, 125

Rocky Butte: 27, 51, 72, 73, *75, 80,* 81

Rooster Rock: 27, 28, 68, *83,* 84, 85

Ross Mountain: 84, 85, 86

Rowena: 72, 105, 106
Rowena Gap fault: 116
Roza Basalt Member: 118
Ruckel landslide: *54*, 56, 98
Ruthton Point: 103, 121

S

Saddle Mountain Basalt: 35, *37*, 38, 70, *107*, 118
Sand dunes: 68, 111
Sandy River: 10, *13, 25*, 28, 46, 47, 69, 73, *75, 78*, 82, 84, *88*, 120
Sandy River Mudstone: 13, 39, 70, 73
Saprolite: 34
Scablands: 45, 106, 109, 111, *112, 114*, 115
Scenic Highway: 64, 67, 82, 97, 103, 105
Sedimentary rocks: 5, 7, *15*, 69, 82, 122
Shellrock Mountain: *ii*, 27, 28, 38, 44, *48*, 51, 71, 99, 101, 102, 123, 124
Shellrock Mountain fault: *48*, 102, 123
Shepperds Dell: 26, 86
Sheridan Point: 127
Shield volcanoes: 11, 18, 23, 24, 69, *75*, 81, 101, 102, 120, 121, 130
Sills: 5, 10
Silver Star Mountain: 131
Skamania Volcanics: 71, *113,* 129, 131, (see also Ohanapecosh)
Spokane floods: 49, 51, 52, 57, 59, 68, 73, *107*, 121, 124, 133 (see also Bretz, Missoula and Glacial floods)
Springwater Formation: 43, 47, 69
Starvation Creek: *26*, 63, 102
Stevenson: 34, 63, 64, 70, *113*, 124, 125
Stevens Ridge Formation: 34, *35*, 71
Stocks: 5, 10, *113*, 131
St. Peters Dome: *9*, 27, 92, 128
Stratification: 8
Stratigraphic column: 3, 4, 12, 17, *35, 43*, 68-71

Stratovolcano: (see composite volcano)
Subduction: 14
Swede Hill: *13*
Synclines: 13, 16, 40, 41, 74, *75*, 84, 115 (see also Hood River, 103; Mosier, 40, 41, *104, 105*, 106, *113, 114*, 118, *119;* Portland, 4, *13*, 16, 40, 70, 74, *75;* The Dalles, 40, 41, 50, 109, 111, 112, *113;* Underwood, 41, 121)

T

Table Mountain: 10, *55*, 70, *94, 96, 113*, 124, 125, *126*
Tanner Butte: 40, 46
Tanner Creek: *25, 26*, 70, *88*, 96, 127
Terraces: 43, 47, 69, 73, *80*, 81, 82, 84, *109*, 115
Tertiary: 2, 24, 32, 33, *43*, 56
The Dalles: xii, 16, 21, 22, 28, 30, 39, 40, 50, 51, 59, 61, 62, 65, 69, 70, *78*, 109, *113, 114*
The Dalles Formation: 4, *35*, 39, 69, 70, 103, *105*, 106, 109, 110, 112, *114*, 118, *119*
The Dalles syncline: 40, 41, 50, 109, 111, 112, *113*
Tooth Rock: 27, 28, 61, 63, *97*, 98
Triassic: 2, 33
Trout Creek Hill: *41, 43*, 99, 124
Troutdale: 24, 47
Troutdale Formation: 4, 12, *13*, 27, 35, 39, 40, 57, 69, 70, 73, *78*, 81, 82, 84, 85, 86, *88*, 89, 92, 96, 99, 102, 103, *113*, 120, 121, 129, 130, 131, 132
Tuff: 6, 7, 70, 71, 103, 120, 121, 128, 132 (see also ash)

U

Umatilla Basin: 50
Unconformity: 5, 8, 9, 122
Underwood Mountain: 4, *41, 43*, 57, 102, *113*, 120, 121, 122
Underwood syncline: 41, 121

V

Vegetation: 30, 44, 86, 103
Viento Creek: 102

Viewpoints: *72,* 73, *76-77,* 84, *85, 105,* 111, 128, 129

Volcaniclastics: 5, 6, 7, 69, 70, 86, 125

W

Wahclella Falls: *26*

Wahkeena Falls: *26,* 89

Wallula Gap: 50

Wanapum Basalt: 35, 37, 38, 70, 85, *107,* 111, 115, 116, 117, 118, 119

Warren Creek: *26*

Washougal River: 28, 62, 71, *113,* 129, 131

Waterfalls: xii, 24, *26,* 28, 51, 64, 65, 70, 86, *88,* 89, *90,* 91, 92, 96, 129

Wauna Point: 127

White Salmon: 4, 28, *41, 43, 113,* 120, 121

Willamette Silts: 43

Willamette syncline: (see Portland syncline)

Wind Mountain: *ii,* 27, 28, 38, 44, 51, 71, *95,* 99, *100,* 101, *113,* 123, 124, 125

Wind Mountain landslide: *54,* 56, *100,* 123

Wind River: 4, 28, *41,* 57, 70, 71, 99, *113,* 124

Y

Yakima Basalt: 3, 4, 9, 10, *13,* 27, *35, 37,* 38, 39, 40, 41, 52, *55,* 69, 70, 73, *78,* 84, 85, *87, 88,* 89, *90,* 92, *94,* 96, *97,* 98, 99, 100, 101, 102, 103, 106, *107, 108, 110,* 111, *113,* 115, 116, *117,* 118, *119, 126,* 131 (see also Grande Ronde, Wanapum and Saddle Mountain Basalts)

Yeon Mountain: 128